A Parent's Guide® to

Philadelphia

Bobbi Dempsey

parent's
guide
press
Los Angeles, CA
www.pgpress.com

A Parent's Guide® to
Philadelphia

Text and Maps © Mars Publishing 2003

ISBN: 1-931199-27-2

This book, and all titles in the Parent's Guide series, are available for purposes of fund raising and educational sales to charity drives, fund raisers, parent or teacher organizations, schools, government agencies and corporations at a discount for purchases of more than 10 copies. Persons or organizations wishing to inquire should call Mars Publishing at 1-800-549-6646 or write to us at *sales@marspub.com*.

At the time of publication of this book, all of the information contained within was correct to the best of our knowledge. If you find information in this book that has changed, please contact us. Even better, if you have additional places to recommend, please let us know. Any included submissions to the new edition of this book will get the submitter a by-line in the book and a free copy of any Mars publication.

Please contact us at *parentsguides@marspub.com*

Printed in Singapore.

parent's guide press

Edwin E. Steussy, CEO and Publisher
Anna-Lisa Fay, Project Editor
Lars H. Peterson, Acquisitions Editor
Michael P. Duggan, Graphic Artist

PO Box 461730
Los Angeles CA 90046

Table of Contents

contents

author's note

Like many other things in my life, I would never have been able to complete this book project without the help, support and encouragement of many people. First, my family—my husband, Jack, and three cool kids, John, Nick, and Brandon, who were my brave accomplices on my research missions around the city. My mother, Marcelle, and sister Marylin also helped with research and planning. My aunts, uncles, and grandmother, Bernice have always been some of my biggest cheerleaders.

I have the privilege of serving as a moderator on a great online group called Momwriters™. Many of the members have become my very good friends, including Nikki, Carma, Anna, and my crew of Philadelphia experts—Mary, Linda, Sue—as well as other great people in this group.

Also, I need to thank the many people, organizations, and businesses that went out of their way to help me gather information about the area. Special thanks to Independence Visitor Center, CityPass, Greater Philadelphia Tourism Marketing Corporation, and www.ushistory.org for their help in compiling information including many of the trivia items and fun facts contained in this book.

Introduction

I may have grown up in the "Big Apple," with its sumptuous New York restaurants; but with my first bite of an authentic Philly cheesesteak from Pat's—which I enjoyed not far from the actual spot where our country's Constitution was signed more than 200 years before—I was hooked.

Amazingly, old and new blend together seamlessly in Philadelphia. This is a town that features both Betsy Ross's house and the incredible, high-tech, four-story domed screen of the Tuttleman IMAX Theater. Not to mention more than four dozen museums, eight professional sports teams, riverboat cruises, and enough stores and shopping malls to satisfy even the most diehard shopaholics.

Many people think Philadelphia has a more casual feel than other big cities like New York and Los Angeles. Plus, the old-fashioned feel of the historic neighborhoods give the town a welcoming atmosphere that many parents really appreciate. As a New York native, I like the attitude (or "addytood," as locals say) of hometown Philly characters. Feisty, yet hard-working and loyal people around here have a disposition that is uniquely Philly. As locals would say, "You gotta problem with that?"

Plus, you can actually spend an enjoyable family trip in Philadelphia without spending a small fortune, a near impossible feat in many other large cities. In fact, you can visit many of the more popular attractions—such as the Liberty Bell, Betsy Ross's house, and the U.S. Mint—without spending a dime.

Like most big cities, Philadelphia does have its attractions, services, and entire neighborhoods that are too expensive, dangerous, or crowded to make for a pleasant family experience. I'll share highlights (and lowlights) from my own Philadelphia experiences along with input from my family and travel-weary parents. My goal is to offer readers of this book much more than the usual "see this, go here" standard travel guide.

Introduction

I'll be sure to include as much feedback and comments from my kids as possible. This is not because I want to mention my kids at every opportunity (although, like any parent, I do), but because my sons have notoriously discriminating taste. So, if an attraction or event earns a "thumbs up" from the Dempsey clan—you can be sure it'll be a hit with your kids, as well.

How to Use This Book

My goal in writing this book was not to give you a dry, boring "tour guide" like the countless others out there. If all you wanted or needed was a directory listing of all there is to do and see in Philly, you can easily get that information just by calling your local travel agent or scouring the Philadelphia phone book. I suspect, like myself and most other parents, when preparing for a family trip, you wish you could get the low-down from other parents familiar with the area. You want to know the real scoop, and hear details that matter to you. It doesn't matter how many fancy restaurants are nearby—I want to know which restrooms have baby-changing stations, so I'm not faced with the prospect of putting poor Junior on a cold concrete floor to change his diaper.

I didn't try to tackle the impossible task of listing every single event, attraction, and any other place of interest in Philly. In fact, I didn't even include every single neighborhood (by some estimates, there are more than 100 individual neighborhoods in the city and its outskirts, each with their own special atmosphere and offerings). Philly is overflowing with many great family-friendly attractions and activities. You are going to have a tough time squeezing even a small fraction of them into one trip; especially if it's only a weekend visit. Most likely, you'll find yourself making repeated returns to Philadelphia and you'll still never run out of things to do. Also, some neighborhoods most likely won't be of interest to families either because there aren't many attractions for children, or because the area is a little too intimidating to venture into if you're not familiar with the environment.

I also wouldn't drag my own kids to some boring exhibit or try to sneak them into a place where kids are definitely frowned upon. I wouldn't lead any trusting readers into those nightmares, either. Sure, like any big city, Philadelphia has lots of trendy hotspots, happening bars and other adult places of interest. But if you were planning to visit the city without kids, you wouldn't be reading this book, now would you? So I've only included places I would take my own kids, and neighborhoods with a family-friendly atmosphere.

Introduction

In the first chapter, I will provide the basic information you need to plan and prepare for your trip around Philadelphia. Since history is such a big part of Philly's allure, I've included some brief historical background and highlights. I've also shared some information on the local climate, and of course maps and guides to help you find the City of Brotherly Love. I will also describe the options for getting around the city.

My aim is to tell you about things that make Philly special and unique, so I won't spend much time on national outlets or other run-of-the-mill places you can find anywhere—unless there's something special about the Philadelphia location. I've also included details on prices, operating hours, and contact information. It is always a good idea to call each place first because the information may have changed.

Philadelphia has so many things to see, do, explore, and experience with your family that it can actually be a little overwhelming, especially if you try to squeeze a whirlwind tour of the entire city into one weekend. It's a much better idea to concentrate on one area of the city at a time, which is why Chapters Two through Six each address a specific section of the city. Rather than give you one enormous listing of every museum in the entire city, I'll tell you lots of things to see, do, eat and enjoy with your kids in a particular neighborhood. So, you can enjoy everything that area has to offer before moving on to another area of the city.

If you have the urge to spread your wings and expand your horizons outside the city limits, Chapter Seven lists great things to see and do in nearby areas. Chapter Eight is a calendar of Philadelphia events (keep in mind that dates and events are subject to change, so again it's a good idea to call beforehand and verify that nothing has changed).

Chapter One

About Philadelphia

Don't be nervous about coming to Philadelphia, even if it's your first visit and you bring the kids along. This is one of the most tourist-friendly towns, from its welcoming attitude to more practical things like plentiful street-top maps that help you figure out where you're headed.

It's very easy to navigate the heart of the city. William Penn designed the city like a grid, so the area is nicely laid out and easy to navigate (the one glitch is mammoth City Hall, which occupies a large section smack dab in the city's center, so you have to go around it to get to the other side of town). The city is comprised of five main districts; each anchored by a square. For example, the Rittenhouse Square district is centered around— you guessed it—Rittenhouse Square. See, I told you it was easy.

The "tree" streets, such as Chestnut, Locust, etc., run east to west. The numbered streets go north and south. Fourteenth Street is called Broad Street, but has recently been renamed Avenue of the Arts. And just in case you get confused, practically every block features a handy directional sign; telling you where you're at and guiding you to some major nearby points of interest.

Chapter One

History

Colonial Days

The Old City section of Philadelphia is often called "America's Most Historic Mile", for good reason. It was here that our nation officially declared its freedom, where our Constitution was created, and where American government as we know it was born.

William Penn founded the city in 1682 and his home—built the same year—was the first brick house built in this country. Penn named his colony Pennsylvania and began to plan the city that is known as Philadelphia—a Greek word meaning City of Brotherly Love. He fashioned the center of this city as a grid; streets running north to south numbered from First to Eighth, and streets running east to west named after trees.

Over the next 100 years or so, many local and national historical highlights occurred in the area. For example, in 1698, the American Colonies' first public school was established in Philadelphia, and in 1704, the First Presbyterian Church was built at Market and Bank streets. In 1723, Ben Franklin arrived in Philadelphia, working as a printer until he and a friend decided to sail to London to seek their fortunes. He returned to Philadelphia in 1726, and in 1731 he and several other men founded the Philadelphia Library—the first public institution of its kind. By 1775, Ben Franklin had become so influential that he was named the first Postmaster General of the United States.

Of course, 1776 was a big year for American history—that's the year when the Declaration of Independence was created, in Philadelphia's Independence Hall. Betsy Ross sewed the first American flag the following year in her Arch Street home.

In 1787, delegates of the thirteen colonies forming the United States met in Philadelphia to unify the new country's governmental structure with the adoption of the U.S. Constitution. Philadelphia, centrally located, was the capital of our country from 1790 to 1800.

About Philadelphia

The Civil War

Philadelphia was the first large city north of the Mason-Dixon line to be involved in the Civil War. The city was home to several regiments of infantry and cavalry who fought for the Union. Thousands of soldiers and sailors were recruited within or near the city. Philadelphia was also one of the main providers of uniforms, munitions, and rifles for the Army. The city's Navy Yard built eleven warships, and many other vessels were fitted for combat during the war. Many troops marched through the city's streets and to the train stations en route to the battlefields. Philadelphia received many of the returning wounded, and the Union set up the first military hospital in the city. Eventually the military hospitals in the city had over 10,000 beds and cared for over 150,000 soldiers and sailors during the war.

The Twentieth Century

The 1950s saw a heavy migration of people and industry to the suburbs and many downtown jobs were lost. Most large cities like Philadelphia were suffering from suburban growth where the suburbs grew faster than the city itself. Many neighborhoods, such as Germantown, East Falls, Queen Village, Bridesburg, Kensington, and Manayunk, would retain the environment of the ethnic groups that initially settled there. Philadelphia engaged in a series of self-improvement plans in the 1950s by replacing blocks of buildings with beautiful parks, modern buildings, and parking garages and by providing better transportation. During this urban renewal, the city lost some significant architecture and Victorian structures. But these improvement plans were an attempt to revitalize the downtown area, and the appearance of downtown changed dramatically with major redevelopment and restoration projects. Some areas that were once industrialized and populated are now open areas for future use. The city of Philadelphia has maintained itself while preserving as much as possible of the old and integrating the new.

Chapter One

Present-Day Philadelphia

Today, Philadelphia is the second largest city on the East Coast and ranks fifth in the nation, with a metropolitan population of 5.8 million. The city truly is a potpourri of all different types of people. Lots of upper income executives call Philly home, as do many college students. The city is home to a "melting pot" of different races, cultures, and ethnic backgrounds.

Coy Butler/Philadelphia Convention & Visitors Bureau

About Philadelphia

Philadelphia Firsts

Philadelphia was the stage for many history-making events, the home of several prominent citizens and statesmen, and the site of some famous landmarks. Over the years, Philadelphia has had many nicknames, such as "Quaker City, Cradle of the Revolution, Nation's Birthplace," and the most enduring, "City of Brotherly Love."

Many U.S. and state "firsts" were associated with the city of Philadelphia:

- America's first public school in 1689
- State's first newspaper in 1719
- Colonies' first public library, established in 1731 by Benjamin Franklin
- America's first volunteer fire company in 1736
- First novel published in America, 1744
- America's first hospital in 1755
- America's first stock exchange in 1746
- America's first fire insurance company in 1752
- America's first life insurance company in 1759
- First Continental Congress in 1774
- First American flag in 1777
- America's first commercial bank, chartered in 1781
- America's first paved turnpike
- First World's Fair in the United States in 1876
- Pennsylvania's first commercial television station in 1941

Chapter One

What You Need to Know about Philadelphia

Location

Philadelphia is on the eastern Pennsylvania border, 100 miles south of New York, 133 miles north of Washington, D.C., and 55 miles from Atlantic City.

Climate

Although we Pennsylvania residents often joke that our state only has two seasons—winter and "Road Work Ahead"—Philadelphia enjoys four distinct seasons with moderately cold winters and hot, humid summers. In January, the average temperature is thirty-three degrees Fahrenheit—temperatures tend to dip below freezing in the evening. In July, the average temperature is seventy-five degrees with sunny, humid days that sometimes approach over ninety degrees Fahrenheit. The average yearly rainfall is forty-one inches; normal seasonal snowfall is twenty-one inches.

Safety

Philadelphia is generally a very safe tourist town; with a heavy law enforcement presence especially in the historic Old City section. However, like many big cities, it does have its share of crime, especially in the economically depressed neighborhoods. For anyone touring the city with kids, I would advise avoiding the regions to the far north or west of Center City, especially at night. I also don't feel comfortable standing with my kids at some of the subway stations at night, so I would suggest limiting subway travel to the daytime hours.

Bring Your Walking Shoes

Philadelphia is definitely a place where you can spend a lot of time on foot. If you're staying in Center City, many of the popular attractions are within walking distance. The city's layout makes it easy to figure out how to get around—the Center City and Old City areas have a flat terrain and wide sidewalks that are a walker's delight.

About Philadelphia

Strollers and Wheelchairs

The city's flat terrain and wide sidewalks make it pretty easy to maneuver strollers and wheelchairs. The only possible snag: a few streets in Old City—such as Elfreth's Alley—still feature the colonial style cobblestone or brick roads. These surfaces make for a bumpy ride.

Get a CityPass!

If you're planning to see some of the most popular Philly attractions, a CityPass can save you considerable time, money, and aggravation. For just $30, the CityPass grants you admission to five different area attractions which save you time and aggravation. If you paid for each attraction separately at the regular price, you'd spend about $60. For example, during one recent visit to the Philadelphia Zoo, the enormous line meant a wait of at least an hour just to get through the gates. Armed with CityPasses, we were able to go through a special entrance and walked right in. To find out more about the CityPass, call (707) 256-0490 or visit www.citypass.com.

Media

Newspapers

- Philadelphia Inquirer
- Philadelphia Daily News
  (Both can be viewed online at www.philly.com)

MetroKids

A great resource for families visiting Philadelphia, MetroKids is a bimonthly newspaper featuring lots of kid-friendly activities and happenings. You can usually find copies of MetroKids at most area malls, libraries, museums, or pick up a copy at the Convention and Visitors Bureau. You can also check out the website at www.metrokids.com.

Radio Stations

AM Stations

610	WIP	Sports
640	WWJZ	Disney
950	WPEN	Adult standard
1340	WHAT	Black-oriented talk
1360	WNJC	News, talk, sports
1370	WPAZ	Easy listening
1420	WCOJ	Talk, adult contemporary
1440	WNPV	News, information

FM Stations

92.1	WVLT	Adult contemporary
92.5	WXTU	Country music
93.3	WMMR	Album-oriented rock
93.7	WSTW	Adult contemporary
94.1	WYSP	Rock
96.5	WPTP	'80s rock
98.9	WUSL	Urban contemporary
99.5	WJBR	Adult contemporary
100.3	WPLY	Modern rock

Useful Phone Numbers

Emergency Numbers

Police/Fire Emergencies—911
Doctor Referral—(215) 563-5343

Airport

Philadelphia International Airport—(215) 937-6937

Bus Companies

Greyhound/Trailways—(800) 231-2222

About Philadelphia

Car Rentals
Alamo—(800) 327-9633
Avis—(800) 331-1212
Budget—(800) 527-0700
Dollar—(800) 800-4000
Hertz—(800) 654-3131
National—(800) 227-7368

Ferry Service
Riverlink Ferry—(215) 925-5465

Area Transit Service
PHLASH—(215) 474-5274

County Convention & Visitors Bureaus

- Bucks County Conference & Visitors Bureau—(800) 836-BUCKS0

- Brandywine Conference & Visitors Bureau—(800) 343-3983

- Lancaster County Convention & Visitors Bureau—(800) PA-DUTCH

- Philadelphia Convention & Visitors Bureau—(800) 537-7676

- Valley Forge/Montgomery County Convention & Visitors Bureau—(800) VISIT-VF

Chapter One

Answers to Philadelphia Questions

Common Questions

- Where are the Rocky steps? **The Philadelphia Museum of Art**

- Where can I research genealogy? **The Balch Institute, the Historical Society of Pennsylvania and, if the ancestor was ever a soldier or received a paycheck from the national government, the National Archives**

- What hotels accommodate pets? **Four Seasons, Loews Hotel, and several bed-and-breakfasts**

Some of the More Unusual—yet Entertaining—Questions

- Where can I find a stable to board my horse? **Fairmount Park**

- Where can I fish in the city? **Schuylkill River**

- Are the Fourth of July fireworks inside or outside? **Outside**

- Where are the stores on Independence Mall? **There are no stores. The word "mall" comes from the English word that referred to a park or place where one could stroll**

Getting Here

By Rail

Philadelphia's Amtrak 30th Street Station is a major East Coast hub, with trains that run along the northeast corridor serving Boston, New York, Baltimore, and Washington.

Amtrak's 30th Street Station is minutes from the Pennsylvania Convention Center and Center City hotels. Local train service is provided by SEPTA, which also connects to NJ Transit trains in Trenton, N.J.

Amtrak—(800) USA-RAIL—www.Amtrak.com

SEPTA—(215) 580-7800—www.septa.org

NJ Transit—(201) 762-5100 (in N.J., 1-800-772-2222)

About Philadelphia

By Plane

Philadelphia International Airport—eight miles from Center City—is served by all major domestic carriers.

By Bus

Intercity bus service is excellent, with daily arrivals from all parts of the country. The Greyhound Bus Terminal is located at 10th and Filbert St.

Greyhound Lines—(215) 931-4075—www.greyhound.com
SEPTA—(215) 580-7800—www.septa.org
Academy Bus Tours—(215) 665-1734

By Car

Philadelphia is served by the PA Turnpike, I-76, I-95, and the New Jersey Turnpike. Directions lead to the Independence Visitor Center in Philadelphia's Old City section.

Note

You have to pay a fee (generally around $3) to cross most of the bridges leading in and out of Philadelphia; so be sure to have some cash with you.

Also, keep in mind that Pennsylvania law requires all passengers to wear seat belts, and children age four and under must be placed in a child safety seat.

Directions

From the South

Take I-95 North. Follow the signs for "Central Phila./I-676" (Exit 22). Follow signs for Phila/Independence Hall/Callowhill Streets. Keep right at the fork in the ramp. Stay straight to Callowhill St. Turn left onto N. 6th Street. The parking facility is directly beneath the building on the left side of 6th Street 1/8 of mile past Arch Street.

From the North

There are three options: NJ Turnpike via Betsy Ross Bridge or Benjamin Franklin Bridge, and I-95.

Chapter One

NJ Turnpike via Benjamin Franklin Bridge

Take the NJ Turnpike to Exit 4. Take Rt. 73 north to Rt. 38 west to US 30. Take US 30 west over the Benjamin Franklin Bridge to I-676. Follow signs for 5th and 6th Street. Stay in the righthand lane. Go past 5th Street exit. Follow signs for Independence Hall/ 6th Street. Make a right at the first light onto Franklin Street. Go around bend. Merge onto 6th Street South. Stay to your left toward 6th Street/ Independence Hall. The parking facility is directly beneath the building on the left side of 6th Street 1/8 of mile past Arch Street.

NJ Turnpike via Betsy Ross Bridge

Take the NJ Turnpike to Exit 4. Take Rt. 73 North to Rt. 90 (Betsy Ross Bridge). Take the Betsy Ross Bridge into Philadelphia. Follow signs for I-95 South (Center City). Take I-95 South. Follow the signs for "Central Phila./I-676" (Exit 22). Follow signs for Phila./Independence Hall/Callowhill Streets. Make right at the light. Stay Straight on Callowhill St. Turn left onto N. 6th Street. The parking facility is directly beneath the building on the left side of 6th Street 1/8 of mile past Arch Street.

Via I-95

Take I-95 South. Follow the signs for "Central Phila./I-676" (Exit 22). Stay to your right. Follow signs for Phila/Independence Hall/Callowhill Streets. Make a right at the light. Stay straight on Callowhill St. Turn left onto N. 6th Street. The parking facility is directly beneath the building on the left side of 6th Street 1/8 of mile past Arch Street.

From the West

Take I-76 (Pennsylvania Turnpike) to the Valley Forge Exit (Exit 326). Follow signs to Philadelphia I-76 East. Remain on I-76 East for about twenty-five miles until you see signs for Central Philadelphia (Exit 344). Continue on 676 East to the 8th Street Exit. Make a right onto 8th Street. Then make a left onto Race Street and a right on 6th Street. The parking facility is directly beneath the building on the left side of 6th Street 1/8 of mile past Arch Street.

About Philadelphia

From the East

Take Atlantic City Expressway to 42 North. Follow 42 North to the Benjamin Franklin Bridge (Rt. 676), crossing into Philadelphia. Follow signs for 5th and 6th Street. Stay in the righthand lane. Go past 5th Street exit. Follow signs for Independence Hall/ 6th Street. Make a right at the first light onto Franklin Street. Go around bend. Merge onto 6th Street South. Stay to your left toward 6th Street/ Independence Hall. The parking facility is directly beneath the building on the left side of 6th Street 1/8 of mile past Arch Street.

The Independence Visitor Center is located on Sixth Street, between Arch and Market Streets, on the left. Metered parking is available on 6th Street. Entrance to a parking garage below the Visitor Center can be found on 6th Street between Arch and Market St.

Driving Times to Philadelphia

- **Atlantic City**—1 hour (62 miles)

- **Boston**—6 hours (320 miles)

- **Buffalo**—7.5 hours (414 miles)

- **New York City**—1.5 hours (90 miles)

- **Trenton, NJ**—45 minutes (35 miles)

- **Washington, DC**—2.5 hours (145 miles)

Tip
Get off the Highway!

Highway traffic surrounding the Philadelphia area can be fast and furious. If you're unsure of which exit you need—or if you simply can't stand highway traffic—it's best to take one of the first Philly exits and find your destination once you get in the city. Since Philly is relatively easy to navigate, it's much easier to get around within the city than trying to spot your exit while in frenzied highway traffic. I was once traveling with a friend who missed her exit and ended up going over the Ben Franklin Bridge (which costs $3 to cross each way). We found ourselves in a less than appealing section of Camden, N.J.

Chapter One

Getting Around

I generally recommend that visitors don't try to navigate the city by car; mostly because there usually is no need, as you have lots of transportation options to get you pretty much anywhere you need to go. Also, most of the roads in Center City are narrow one-way streets that can be challenging even to local drivers. Plus, parking garages can be expensive and street parking can be almost impossible to find. Of course, there are the usual big-city concerns of finding a safe place to park and hoping your car (and all of its parts and contents) will actually still be there when you return.

However, if you insist on driving around town, here are some pointers:

The Kelly Drive (East River Drive) and the West River Drive are both scenic routes that border the Schuykill River; nice to use for a more leisurely drive into town. However, on Sundays the West River Drive is closed to traffic. It is open for recreational use only. You'll find people skateboarding, bicycling, rollerblading, and walking all along there on Sundays.

At publication time, parts of I-95 toward Northeast Philly, as well as I-76 at King of Prussia, were under construction. While this project will (hopefully) be completed by the time you read this book, construction is very common in the area; so chances are you'll encounter several work areas in or around the city. Basically, it's best to always anticipate some delays and plan accordingly. I-76 near downtown Philly is always congested at rush hour. The sports complex area is always congested during sporting and concert events, so avoid driving Broad Street during these times—use the subway or Septa bus service to get to these events.

Most Center City streets run one-way, with traffic on "even" streets (2nd Street, 4th Street, etc.) going south and traffic on odd streets heading north, so it is fairly easy to plot your route and keep oriented. When looking for a specific address, remember that each block occupies a 100-number interval, with the north-south crosspoint being Market Street. For example, to find 340 S. 4th Street, you'd head south on 4th Street, and look in the area between three and four blocks south of Market. It helps to plan your route in advance, as this area is very congested on weekdays, especially during rush hour.

About Philadelphia

Fun Facts

- 2,800 traffic signs
- 15,000 stop intersections
- 3,000 all-way stop intersections
- 100,000 street lights
- 18,000 alley lights

Phlash

www.phillyphlash.com

My absolute favorite way to get around Philadelphia is the Phlash shuttle buses, operated by the city's SEPTA transit system. I cannot tell you how easy the Phlash system makes it to get from place to place, or to just take a sightseeing tour of the city. In fact, many locals actually use the Phlash to get back and forth to work downtown, as it's much cheaper than paying the steep inner-city parking fees. Every major city should have a system similar to the Phlash. They're different from run-of-the-mill city buses because they go in a continuous loop around the city, stopping only at thirty-four designated points around the city. (Look for the "wings" Phlash sign on corners.) Plus, the shuttles' on-board computer system provide a running commentary as you pass or stop at various attractions. More importantly, the drivers are among the friendliest and most helpful employees you will ever meet. On one occasion, we were going from the Doubletree Hotel to the Philadelphia Zoo. Since we boarded at the 32nd stop on the route, it would normally take about a half-hour to go through the loop and get to the zoo (Stop #24). However, the driver pointed out that we could get off at Stop #1 (the Convention Center) and just cross the street to catch another Phlash at Stop #18, thus eliminating a huge chunk of travel time. At just $10 for an all-day pass (which covers a family of up to 5 people), it's a deal that can't be beat. Best of all, you save the hassle and expense of finding parking at every attraction. Exact fare is required. Buses run every ten minutes from 10:00 a.m. to 6:00 p.m., and until midnight during the summer.

Tip

It's best not to try and get the first 10:00 a.m. bus, especially if you're boarding toward the end of the route, as the bus is often filled to capacity. Better to get a bite to eat and wait about twenty minutes, when the buses will be nice and roomy.

SEPTA

(215) 580-7853

In addition to the Phlash shuttles mentioned above, the city's transit system gets you around by bus, train, subway, and trolley. Just about any attraction, historic or cultural site, entertainment venue, hotel, restaurant, or event in Center City can be reached by a handful of SEPTA services. These include the Regional Rail R1 Airport Line; the Market-Frankford Line (serving east-west destinations); the Broad Street Line (serving north-south destinations); Bus Routes 21, 38, and 42; Spree, the shoppers' shuttle; PHLASH, the downtown visitor shuttle; and LUCY, the loop through University City.

Exact change is required. The best buy is a SEPTA day pass, which will give you unlimited use of all SEPTA vehicles for the entire day. At publication time, a day pass cost $5.50. You can even buy passes online at www.septa.org.

Like the subways in other big cities, the one in Philly doesn't exactly have that "clean and comforting" feeling. Generally, when traveling with kids, I prefer the above-ground methods of getting around the city.

Tip

In September 2002, KYW Newsradio and SEPTA kicked off a year-long promotion called "Free Ride Tuesdays." KYW will provide free SEPTA service aboard the Big Blue Bus—a forty foot vehicle is wrapped in blue with the KYW logo in white letters on the side—every Tuesday until September 2003. The Big Blue Bus will operate on different routes throughout SEPTA's service region. Passengers may ride the Big Blue Bus for free on Tuesdays only, and only the KYW bus will offer free rides each Tuesday. Riders traveling on other buses on that route will be responsible for the regular SEPTA fare. KYW Newsradio will announce the route that the Big Blue Bus will operate on each Tuesday in on-air promotions.

Taxis

The taxi companies are really just dispatching services. Each individual cab is owned by the driver, so quality, service, and cleanliness varies greatly from one cab to another. For areas outside center city, it's best to call for a cab—otherwise, you might have a wait. Compared to other available forms of transportation in Philly, cabs are a pretty pricey way to get around.

- **City Cab Co.**—(215) 492-6500
- **Liberty Cab Co.**—(215) 389-8000
- **Olde City Taxi Coach Assoc.**—(215) AIRPORT
- **Quaker City Cab**—(215) 728-8000

About Philadelphia

Horse-Drawn Carriage

If you really want to get a taste of colonial life, what better way to get around than by horse-drawn carriage? Tours are available by calling the '76 Trolley Company at (215) 923-8516.

By Foot

There are so many things to see on practically every block of Center City and Old City Philadelphia that walking is actually one of the best choices to get around without missing any of the sites. The area is very pedestrian-friendly and is perfectly tailored to travel by foot. Plus, if you walk, you won't be annoyed by the fact that almost every street is a "one way," and driving somewhere often involves going in a big circle around your destination in order to accommodate the street layouts.

Shopping

Philadelphia is a shopaholic's paradise, with a seemingly endless array of retail establishments ranging from cozy boutiques to huge shopping malls. I've listed stores and malls of interest according to their location, but here are a few things to keep in mind:

- **Philadelphia sales tax is 7%**, which is charged on everything but clothing.

- **The first Friday of every month is a special day for shoppers.** On that day, stores in the Old City section remain open until 9:00 p.m. and offer refreshments for weary shoppers.

Famous Philly Foods

Cheesesteaks

The ultimate Philly food, a cheesesteak, consists of strips or thin slices of steak, which are fried (often in onions) and then heaped onto a big hoagie roll, then topped with cheddar, provolone, or Cheese Whiz. Not to be confused with a hoagie, also called a sub, which consists of cold lunch meat.

- **Jim's Steaks**, 401 South Street—(215) 928-1911
- **Pat's King of Steaks**, 1011 E. Passyunk Avenue—(215) 468-1546

Water Ice

Also known as Italian Ice, this refreshing treat is flavored shaved ice, usually served in a paper cone.
- **Rita's Water Ice**, 235 South Street—(215) 629-3910
- **John's Water Ice**, 702 Christian Street—(215) 925-6955
- **Philadelphia Water Ice Factory Inc.**, 4322 Bermuda Street—(215) 533-0400
- **Morrone's Water Ice**, 200 N. 63rd Street—(215) 747-2909
- **Dati's Delight**, 2335 S. Hemberger Street (at 23rd & Passyunk)—(215) 271-0186

Tastykakes—a Philadelphia Tradition

Tastykake makes cupcakes and pastries to please any taste bud. I'm fond of the butterscotch Krimpets, while my kids tend to gobble up the peanutbutter Kandykakes.
- **The Tastykake Baking Company**, 29th & Allegheny Avenue—(800) 33-TASTY

Soft Pretzels

These hot salted treats are usually served topped with mustard or cheese.
- **The Pretzel Museum**, 211 N 3rd Street—(215) 413-3010

About Philadelphia

Top Ten Places to Photograph Your Kids

(According to Bob Krist, a photographer with a large file of Philadelphia photography—www.bobkrist.com)

1. On the steps of the Art Museum (doing the famous "Rocky run")
2. Sitting next to Ben Franklin at Franklin Court
3. Aboard the RiverLink Ferry with Philly in the background
4. In front of the LOVE sculpture at Love Park
5. In front of the walk-through heart at the Franklin Institute
6. In front of Independence Hall
7. Posing as *The Thinker* statue in front of the Rodin Museum
8. Sitting with their feet in the Swann Fountain
9. Eating a big cheesesteak at Pat's Steaks
10. Juggling produce at the Italian Market

Fun & Free in Philly

Like many parents, one of the things I dread most about family vacations is the budget-busting cost. Fortunately, Philadelphia offers many fun attractions that don't cost a cent. Here are some highlights (detailed descriptions of each can be found throughout this book):

- Congress Hall
- Carpenters' Hall
- Elfreth's Alley Museum
- Fairmount Park
- Franklin Mint Museum
- Liberty Bell Pavilion
- Independence Hall
- City Hall Tower, Exhibit and Observation Deck
- Rodin Museum
- U.S. Mint
- Fireman's Hall Museum
- Old City Hall

Chapter One

Where to Stay

Doubletree Hotel

Broad and Locust Streets
Philadelphia, PA 19107
(215) 893-1600

The Doubletree's cool design lets each room have a "corner" view of Center City. The pool area leads onto the fourth-story courtyard, where you can watch all of the activity below. The staff is wonderful, and will gladly set you up in adjoining rooms so the kids can have their own space.

Rittenhouse Hotel

210 W. Rittenhouse Square
Philadelphia, PA 19103
(215) 546-9000

This beautiful hotel features a gorgeous lobby complete with marble floor and crystal chandeliers. Yet it's surprisingly kid-friendly; they have many events (including cooking classes!) just for kids.

Hawthorn Suites

1100 Vine Street
Philadelphia, PA 19107
(215) 829-8300

Conveniently located near Chinatown and the Reading Terminal Market, these suites are perfect for families who want to be close to the action.

Hotel Windsor

1700 Benjamin Franklin Parkway
Philadelphia PA 19103
(215) 981-5678

Located in the museum district, the Windsor features suites with kitchen facilities, plus a pool and two restaurants.

Philadelphia Marriott

12th and Market Streets
Philadelphia, PA 19107
(215) 625-2900

A huge hotel near the Convention Center, the Marriott features an indoor pool, a beautiful five-story lobby and a special kids' menu from room service.

About Philadelphia

Hyatt Regency at Penn's Landing

201 S. Columbus Blvd.
Philadelphia, PA 19106
(215) 928-1234

The Hyatt Regency at Penn's Landing really goes out of its way to create a child-friendly/child safe environment. The hotel's ten childproof suites include cordless curtains, sealed windows, tethered lamps and wires, corner protectors on tables, protected electrical outlets, baby gates, toilet locks, skid-proof bathtubs and a video library. The best feature—the children's menu at Keating's Restaurant is on the back of an Etch-A-Sketch board!

Best Western at Independence Park Inn

235 Chestnut Street
Philadelphia, PA 19106
(215) 922-4443

The hotel has thirty-six guest rooms, including deluxe suites containing king-sized beds and parlors. You can rent VCRs and videos for an extra charge.

Holiday Inn Express Midtown

1305 Walnut Street
Philadelphia, PA 19107
(215) 735-9300

An affordable hotel with a great location—close to shopping, theaters and lots of other Philly attractions.

Four Seasons

One Logan Square
Philadelphia, PA 19103
(215) 963-1500
www.fourseasons.com

Okay, this is definitely not for those with a tight budget, but if you really want to indulge and get a taste of the "good life" while in Philadelphia, you'll feel like royalty at the Four Seasons. To my surprise, this hotel is actually very kid-friendly—children get milk and cookies at bedtime, which they can enjoy while playing in-room video games. Even small pets get the royal treatment, with decorative dog treats and sparkling water served in a fancy bowl. The hotel often runs special deals for families, which can help make your stay a little more reasonably priced.

Chapter One

Korman Suites Hotel

2001 Hamilton Street
Philadelphia, PA 19130
(215) 569-7000

If you want all the comforts of home, this hotel offers many suites with washers and dryers, kitchen appliances, and more. It's located in the museum district, but you can easily take the PHLASH to all the Center City attractions.

Sheraton Society Hill Hotel

One Dock Street
Philadelphia, PA 19106
(215) 238-6000

A little on the pricey side, but it has a great location near Penn's Landing and Independence Hall. Also, an indoor pool, which is something I always look for a good back-up way to keep kids happy, if the weather gets bad.

Chapter Two

Historic District

This is generally the first—and sometimes the only—destination for Philadelphia visitors. The historic region's Old City is home to many of Philly's most famous landmarks—the Liberty Bell, Betsy Ross's house, Independence Hall, and lots more. You just can't help but feel patriotic while walking "America's Most Historic Mile." But just to be sure, the colonial re-enactors strolling the area are sure to put you in the right frame of mind.

The Historic District also includes Society Hill, Penn's Landing, and Franklin Square.

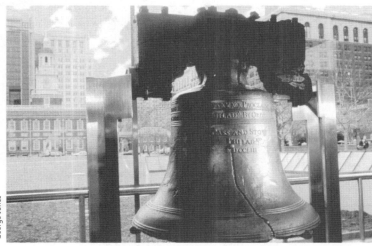
George Jones

Chapter Two

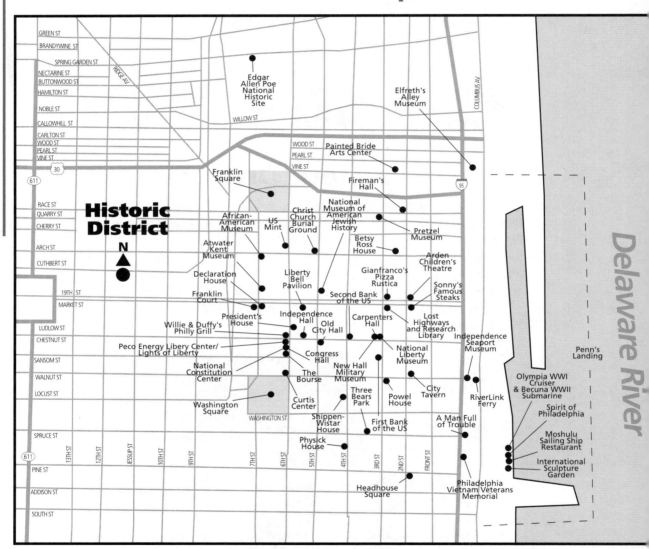

GREEN ST
BRANDYWINE ST
SPRING GARDEN ST
NECTARINE ST
BUTTONWOOD ST
HAMILTON ST
NOBLE ST
CALLOWHILL ST
CARLTON ST
WOOD ST
PEARL ST
VINE ST

RIDGE AV

WILLOW ST

COLUMBUS AV

30

611

US
95

RACE ST
QUARRY ST
CHERRY ST

ARCH ST

CUTHBERT ST

Historic District

N

19TH ST
MARKET ST

LUDLOW ST
CHESTNUT ST

SANSOM ST

WALNUT ST

LOCUST ST

SPRUCE ST

611

13TH ST
12TH ST
JESSUP ST
10TH ST
9TH ST
7TH ST
6TH ST
5TH ST
4TH ST
3RD ST
2ND ST
FRONT ST

PINE ST

ADDISON ST

SOUTH ST

Edgar Allen Poe National Historic Site

Elfreth's Alley Museum

Painted Bride Arts Center

Franklin Square

Fireman's Hall

African-American Museum

US Mint

Christ Church Burial Ground

National Museum of American Jewish History

Pretzel Museum

Atwater Kent Museum

Betsy Ross House

Declaration House

Liberty Bell Pavilion

Gianfranco's Pizza Rustica

Arden Children's Theatre

Franklin Court

Second Bank of the US

Sonny's Famous Steaks

President's House

Independence Hall

Old City Hall

Carpenters Hall

Lost Highways and Research Library

Independence Seaport Museum

Willie & Duffy's Philly Grill

Peco Energy Libery Center/ Lights of Liberty

Congress Hall

National Liberty Museum

Penn's Landing

National Constitution Center

The Bourse

New Hall Military Museum

City Tavern

Olympia WWI Cruiser & Becuna WWII Submarine

Curtis Center

Three Bears Park

Powel House

RiverLink Ferry

Spirit of Philadelphia

Washington Square

WASHINGTON ST

Shippen-Wistar House

First Bank of the US

A Man Full of Trouble

Moshulu Sailing Ship Restaurant

Physick House

International Sculpture Garden

Headhouse Square

Philadelphia Vietnam Veterans Memorial

Delaware River

Historic District

HPI Gazette

The HPI Gazette is the official newsletter of Historic Philadelphia, Inc. Pick up the latest copy at the Visitors Center or one of dozens of locations throughout the district—or visit www.historicphiladelphia.org to get yours online. *The Gazette* features:

- **The latest news** about upcoming events
- **A full program** schedule
- **A colorful map** of Philadelphia's historic district
- **Contact information and operating hours** for Philadelphia's leading historic attractions
- **Plus dozens of ideas** to make your stay in historic Philadelphia more exciting!

Old City

www.oldcitydistrict.org

Old City is the section roughly from Front to Fifth Streets between Walnut and Arch. In addition to historical landmarks and attractions, Old City boasts more than forty art galleries, fifty retail establishments, over forty restaurants, eight hotels, twenty-five museums, two theaters, and three movie theaters.

By day, this area is swarming with tourists (casual dress is fine, and comfy shoes are a must). A heavy police presence (a combination of city police, National Park Service rangers and other personnel) gives the area a very safe feeling. Despite the large number of daily visitors, the area remains clean and well maintained, partly due to daily street sweeping and constant maintenance. After dark, the area's nightlife really heats up. Not that I would know firsthand since we're usually tucked into bed long before this hour, but I hear these streets can get a little rowdy around 2:00 a.m., after "last call" at all the local bars. However, the constant presence of security personnel makes this the safest section of the entire city.

Chapter Two

Directions

By Subway

Take the Market-Frankford (blue) line to 2nd & Market Streets.

By Bus

Running east/west on Market Street:
#17, #33, #48, #76, #121, #44
Running east on Chestnut Street: #9, #21, #42

By PATCO High Speed Line

Take PATCO to 8th & Market Streets. Transfer to the Market-Frankford line, heading east to 2nd & Market Streets.

By Train

Take the R1-8 trains to Market East Station. Transfer to the Market-Frankford Line, heading east to 2nd & Market Streets.

Take Amtrak to 30th Street Station. Transfer to the Market-Frankford Line, heading east to 2nd & Market Streets.

Historic District

Independence Visitor Center

Sixth and Market Streets
One North Independence Mall West
Philadelphia, PA 19106
(215) 597-8974
www.independencevisitorcenter.com

Any tour of Philadelphia should begin with a stop at the Independence Visitors Center. It's officially located at Sixth and Market Streets, but since it occupies several square blocks, it's also listed as Third and Chestnut Streets, or some other variation. It's part of the Independence National Historic Park cluster, which also includes the Liberty Bell Pavilion and Independence Hall.

Before you set off to explore historical Philly, take a few moments to watch the movie *Independence* here to get you in the right mood. You can also make reservations for area attractions through their ticketing service, and load up on more maps, brochures, flyers, and other informative stuff that you'll be able to carry. You can also sign up to join an organized tour provided by the Neighborhood Tourism Network. The trolley tours last about three hours, cost between $20 and $30, and have themes such as "Murals, Mummers & Mozzarella" and "Latin Soul."

Independence Visitor Center

Cost: Free

Directions: Take Market Street west from Center City until you reach Sixth. All major forms of Philly travel (trolley, bus and PHLASH) stop right at the corner.

Parking: The Autopark at Independence Mall is open 24 hours with entrances at 6th and 5th Streets between Market and Arch Streets. Rates begin at $2 per half-hour, with various special deals available.

Independence Visitors Center Tip
The *Magna Carta* will be on display here through spring 2003.

Edward Savaria Jr/Convention & Visitors Bureau

Independence Visitors Center

Chapter Two

Or have one of the Visitor Center guides (dressed in traditional colonial wear) help you plan a route of your own. These guides (my kids refer to each of the men as "the Ben Franklin guy" and the women are all dubbed "that Betsy Ross lady") seem to be walking encyclopedias on the area and its history. Trust me, if you've got a question that's in any way related to Philadelphia, these are the people to ask.

During peak tourist season (March-October) you also need to stop at the Visitor Center to pick up your free tickets to tour the nearby attractions like Independence Hall and the Liberty Bell Pavilion. The Visitor Center offers concierge service for trip-planning assistance, and is also home to Independence Store and Old Capital Coffee. You can purchase CityPass booklets, Phlash passes and other tickets for local attractions here. Oh, and you'll be thrilled to know that both the men's and woman's restrooms have baby-changing stations (I love equal-opportunity diaper duty!).

Fun Facts

- **Most expensive souvenir at Independence Store: replica of Independence Hall ($110). Least expensive souvenir: replicas of Continental money ($1.50).**

- **Most unusual gifts: glass barometer, a rain stick and corn husk dolls.**

- **Millennium Coffee, a Philadelphia-based coffee purveyor, created "Liberty Brew," a special blend served at the Independence Visitor Center coffee bar.**

Historic District

Independence National Historic Park

Third Street, between Chestnut and Walnut
Philadelphia, PA 19106
(215) 597-8974
www.nps.gov/inde/

Although security was always important at INHP, safety measures have increased considerably since the terrorist attacks because of the area's national historic significance. The security procedures outlined below—while said to be only temporary—were still in place as of publication time.

Independence National Historic Park

Hours: Daily, dawn to dusk

Most park buildings are open daily from 9:00 a.m. to 5:00 p.m. in the summer, the hours of some buildings are extended. You can obtain seasonal information on park hours of operation and park programs by calling the Visitor Center at (215) 597-8974.

Cost: Free

Directions: The INHP is right across the street from the Visitor Center. It is Stop #5 on the Phlash route.

A new security screening facility, located on Fifth Street between Market and Chestnut Streets, will serve as a single entry point for visitors to the historic icons. INHP will also close a pedestrian walkway on the 500 block of Chestnut Street to create a single security zone.

Visitors will need to go through the security process only once, rather than at two locations. Previously, visitors went through metal detectors and package inspections at both the Liberty Bell Pavilion and Independence Hall. The screening facility will open at 8:30 a.m. daily, to screen visitors who wish to enter the buildings starting at 9:00 a.m. The last visitors will be screened at 4:45 p.m.

Also, cell phone, beepers and other noisy electronic devices must be turned off the entire time you are within the Independence Park area.

Chapter Two

Liberty Bell Pavilion
Market Street, between 5th and 6th Streets
(215) 597-8974

Coy Butler/Philadelphia Convention & Visitors Bureau

Liberty Bell Pavilion
Hours: Daily 9 am- 5 pm
Ages: 3 and up
Cost: Free
Directions: Adjacent to the INHP

Interestingly, the Liberty Bell, which was cast in 1751, was originally called the State House Bell. It was rung to beckon Philadelphians to Independence Square for the first reading of the Declaration of Independence on July 4, 1776. But it didn't crack then. Instead, it slowly cracked over a period of years, was repaired and then cracked again to be silenced forever in 1846.

Under usual circumstances, a bell that no longer rings is taken down from the belfry, melted down, and used for other purposes. In this case, however, a group of Abolitionists, inspired by the bell's inscription, which reads "to proclaim liberty throughout all the land unto all the inhabitants thereof," rechristened it the "Liberty Bell" and publicized its role in our nation's birth as part of their argument that all Americans—including slaves—should be free.

A park ranger gives a short, yet informative speech during your visit to the Liberty Bell Pavilion.

Historic District

Independence Hall

Chestnut Street between 5th and 6th Streets
(215) 597-8974

The site where the Declaration of Independence and the U.S. Constitution were signed, and the Articles of Confederation were drafted. Tour guides generally make sure kids and other "height-challenged" people get a spot up front during tours of the various rooms.

Coy Butler/Philadelphia Convention & Visitors Bureau

Independence Hall

Hours: Daily, 9 am- 5 pm
Closed Christmas and New Year's Day

Ages: 7 and up

Cost: Free

Fun Facts about Independence Hall

- The basement once served as the city's dog pound.

- The second floor was once home to Charles Wilson Peale's museum of natural history.

- Some historians note that Ben Franklin would occasionally trip other delegates from his aisle seat.

- George Washington, knowing that his opinion would carry undue weight, contributed little to the debate over the Constitution.

- Even though the days were very hot in the summer of 1787, windows were kept closed so others could not overhear their discussions.

Chapter Two

President's House
Sixth Street, between Chestnut and Market

This house (actually, the house that once stood in this spot) was the Executive Mansion of the United States from 1790 to 1800 during Philadelphia's tenure as the national capital. George Washington and John Adams each lived and worked here for most of their presidencies. The house stood one block north of Independence Hall. A public bathroom has occupied the site for the past forty-eight years.

The National Park Service plans to erect a new building for the Liberty Bell on the property, although this has met with some controversy because the proposed site would have the Liberty Bell sitting almost directly atop the spot where Washington housed his slaves. Future visitors will walk across the entire footprint of the main house, kitchen, and slave quarters on their way to the new building.

Fun Facts about President's House

- While living in this house, Benedict Arnold began his treasonous correspondence with the British.
- General Howe lived in this house during the occupation by the British in 1777.
- Financier Robert Morris purchased the house in 1785. He rented the house to Washington and Adams.

Edgar Allen Poe National Historic Site

532 North Seventh Street
Philadelphia, PA 19123
Phone: (215) 597-8780
www.fieldtrip.com/pa/55978780.htm

> **Edgar Allen Poe National Historic Site**
>
> Hours: 9 am-5 pm daily
>
> Cost: free
>
> Directions: From Market Street, take Seventh Street north about six blocks.

This site consists of three buildings and a park area. Poe rented several Philadelphia homes during his lifetime, but this small brick house is the only one remaining. No one seems to know what happened to his belongings, but you can tour the empty home. The house is appropriately (though unintentionally) creepy, with its peeling paint and creaky floors. My kids liked the Junior Ranger activity books they received during our last visit here. This is an especially popular spot during October, when Halloween "ghost tours" are held here.

Historic District

Washington Square

Between 6th and 7th Streets and Walnut and Locust

One of the "five squares," this was the hot spot in the area before the INHP set up shop. The square once served as a burial ground for victims of Yellow Fever. It also contains the Tomb of the Unknown Soldier, a memorial to honor unidentified victims of the Revolutionary War. It's a great place to relax, people-watch or plan your next walking tour. Unfortunately, it's also popular with the pigeons, so keep alert!

Tours

American Jewish Committee Historic Tours

117 S. 17th Street, Suite 1010
Philadelphia, PA 19103
(215) 665-2300

This tour of historic Philadelphia sights with Jewish history behind each stop is full of humor and insight into our past.

Connective Tours

1119 N. Bodine Street
Philadelphia, PA 19123
(215) 925-TOUR

Guided tours of Historic Philadelphia by trolley, motorcoach, and horse-drawn carriage. Day tours are offered to Lancaster, Washington, and New York.

Ghost Tours of Philadelphia

Tours begin at 5th and Chestnut Streets
(215) 413-1997

Hear the haunting tales of America's most historic—and most haunted city on this candlelight walking tour. Fun for all ages. Call for times, location, ticket sales, and reservations.

Chapter Two

Philadelphia Hospitality, Inc.

123 S. Broad Street, Suite 1330
Philadelphia, PA 19109
(215) 790-9901
(800) 714-3287

This private, nonprofit organization arranges unique, multiday cultural programs for groups visiting the Greater Philadelphia region. Take a behind-the-scenes look at cultural and historical treasures, visit private homes, exquisite gardens, and private clubs.

Philadelphia Open House

313 Walnut Street
Philadelphia, PA 19106
(215) 928-1188

Rare and intimate glimpses into private homes, gardens and special places featuring architecture, interior design, and historic preservation achievements. Some tours include transportation—call for details.

Philadelphia Trolley Works

1119 N. Bodine Street
Philadelphia, PA 19123
(215) 925-TOUR

Narrated trolley tour with all day on/off privileges.

Poor Richard's Walking Tours

PO Box 8193
Philadelphia, PA 19101
(215) 206-1682

Poor Richard's offers walking tours of the city of Philadelphia, led by professional scholars and teachers in the field of history. The guides are primarily graduate students at the University of Pennsylvania, located in West Philadelphia. Walking tours include: Colonial Philadelphia, the Nineteenth Century City, Ethnic Philadelphia: Chinatown to South Philadelphia, West Philadelphia: Past & Present, the University of Pennsylvania & Environs, and the Streetcar Suburb.

Historic District

Trophy Bike Tours

311 Market Street
Philadelphia, PA 19106
(215) 625-7999

Easy-paced one-to-three hour bicycle tours: See all of Philadelphia's beauty and history up close. Modern bikes, and skilled cycle guides are available.

Mural Tours

There are more than 2,100 indoor and outdoor murals in Philadelphia—way too many to list here, of course. The best way to check out some of the murals—aside from just strolling around town and discovering them by chance—is to take a mural tour. Tours depart Saturdays at 11:00 a.m. at the Independence Visitor Center at 6th and Market Streets. Each week features the murals of a different Philadelphia neighborhood. Please call (215) 685-0754 for information about upcoming tours. For more information about the murals in Philly, visit www.muralarts.org.

Edward Savaria Jr/ Philadelphia Convention & Visitors Bureau

Chapter Two

National Museum of American Jewish History

55 North 5th Street
Philadelphia, PA 19106
(215) 923-3811
www.nmajh.org

This museum offers education, exhibits, and programs dedicated to preserving the history and culture of the Jewish people in America.

> **National Museum of American Jewish History**
>
> Hours: Mon-Thurs, 10 am-5 pm; Fri, 10 am-3 pm; Sun, 12 pm-5 pm; Closed Sat.
>
> Cost: Adults $4; Children (6-7) $3
>
> Directions: From the Liberty Bell, take Fifth Street up a block towards Arch.

Franklin Court

314-22 Market Street
(215) 597-8974

Franklin's house is no longer standing, but you can get a good idea of what it looked like by checking out the "Ghost House" designed by Robert Venturi and located in the same spot where Franklin's house once stood. You can also tour the underground museum of Franklin's inventions, as well as a reconstructed eighteenth century print shop.

> **Franklin Court**
>
> Hours: Daily, 9 am-5 pm; with some exceptions. Call to verify.
>
> Cost: Free
>
> Directions: One block north of the Visitor Center.

As you enter the Court (which is accessed via an alley from Chestnut Street or through the row houses on Market Street), you'll see steel frames that mark the sites of Franklin's "good house" and his grandson's printing office and type foundry (both Benjamin Franklin and his grandson, Benjamin Franklin Bache, were printers when they were young). The original buildings were destroyed in 1812 and not enough information survived to re-create them. So instead, the steel silhouettes (sometimes called "ghosts") were built to suggest the presence of the eighteenth century brick buildings.

The underground museum contains exhibits telling all about Franklin's various inventions and achievements. My kids get a kick out of the "Franklin Exchange," where you can pick up a phone and call someone that Franklin knew and listen to what their conversation might have sounded like.

Also, be sure to bring your mail to the B. Free Franklin Post Office at 316 Market Street, where you can get it hand-stamped with Franklin's signature.

Historic District

Peco Energy Liberty Center/ Lights of Liberty

6th and Chestnut Streets
(877) GO2-1776
www.lightsofliberty.org

**Peco Energy Liberty
Center/Lights of Liberty**

Hours: Mon-Sat; 10 am-10
pm; Sun 11 am-4 pm.

Ages: 6 and up

Cost: Adults $17.76;
Children (under 12) $12

The story of the Revolution is told through beautiful hand-painted images that are projected up to fifty feet high onto the buildings where the events actually took place over 200 years ago. This is very cool, and I challenge anyone to walk away from this without feeling extremely patriotic!

Five story projections on historic buildings and wireless headsets equipped with 3D sound make it all seem real. Shows take place throughout Independence National Historical Park.

Jim McWilliams/Philadelphia Convention & Visitors Bureau

41

Chapter Two

Living History

Historic Philadelphia (HPI) Re-Enactments

123 Chestnut Street
Suite 401
Philadelphia, PA 19106
(215) 629-5801 or toll free (800) 76-HISTORY
www.historicphiladelphia.org

Historic re-enactors take to the streets of Philadelphia to welcome visitors. HPI performs numerous performances each week, including a new play about Betsy Ross. Throughout the day, Colonial Townspeople—actors portraying everyday eighteenth century Philadelphia residents—discuss their lives and answer questions about life during that time period. During the summer months, performers act out the Living History Program. I'm fond of the LibertyTones, a singing troupe that wanders the historical area performing authentic colonial selections. My kids, meanwhile, are still getting over the horrible image invoked by one re-enactor who pointed out that there were no video games or televisions during colonial times.

United States Mint

151 North Independence Mall East
Philadelphia, PA 19106-1886
(215) 597-7350
www.usmint.gov

Tours of the U.S. Mint, which were suspended following Sept. 11, were resuming as of publication time. Call for the current status and schedule of tours.

My kids always have to make sure to say hello to "Peter the Mint Eagle," who presides over the Mint's entrance. According to legend, Peter was a friendly bird who spent evenings soaring around the first Mint building on 7th Street. Poor Peter supposedly met a tragic fate when a machine started unexpectedly as he was perched on it.

United States Mint

Hours: July-Aug:
Mon-Fri, 9 am-4:30 pm;
Sat, 9 am-4:30 pm;
Sun, 11 am-4:30 pm;
rest of year, open
only on weekdays.

Ages: 7 and up

Cost: Free

Directions: From the
Liberty Bell, take Fifth
Street two blocks
north to Race.

Historic District

Fun Facts

- Today there are four United States mints: Philadelphia, Denver, San Francisco, and West Point. The bullion depository at Fort Knox is also part of the Mint system.

- On October 19, 1995—a typical day—the mint produced 30 million coins worth about one million dollars.

- The Philadelphia facility is the largest mint in the world.

- At the original Mint, a lone night watchman armed with a sword, pistol, and watchdog was responsible for security.

- George and Martha Washington donated the silver that was used to make the first coins.

- Baseball fans will appreciate that the voice you hear when you press the buttons on the self-guided tour belongs to the voice of the Phillies' Harry Kalas.

The Bourse

111 S. Independence Mall East
Philadelphia, PA 19106
(215) 625-0300

The Bourse

Directions: Across the street from the Liberty Bell on Fifth.

The Bourse Building opened in 1865, and originally served as home of several commerce departments, including the Maritime Exchange and the Commercial Exchange. Some offices still occupy the upper floors, but the big attractions are the large food court and tourist shops.

Check out the Grande Olde Cheesesteak and order the sandwich of the same name; it comes complete with sweet Italian peppers, lettuce, tomatoes, sautéed mushrooms and your choice of cheddar, American or Provolone cheese. I swear, whoever created this cheesesteak had my husband in mind. My kids, on the other hand, would rather have a bottle of Hank's Philadelphia rootbeer.

While they're chowing down, I usually hit the stores. At **The Best of Philadelphia**, I stock up on their large selection of T-shirts. If I feel like splurging, I head to **Making History**, which is a bit pricier, but features some really cute teddy bears and other upscale items.

Chapter Two

Betsy Ross House

239 Arch Street
Philadelphia, PA 19106
(215) 627-5343

Betsy and her husband, John, rented this little house and ran their upholstery business here from 1773 to 1786. Glassed-in rooms with mannequins give kids a good sense of how people lived and dressed.

Betsy Ross House

Hours: Memorial Day through Labor Day—
Daily, 10 am-5 pm;
Winter—Tues-Sun, 10 am-5 pm

Closed on Thanksgiving, Christmas, and New Year's Day; open on Monday holidays (Martin Luther King Day, Presidents' Day, Columbus Day, Veteran's Day).

Cost: Adults $2; Children $1

Directions: From Visitor Center, take Third Street three blocks north.

After her death, the property went through a series of owners, but in 1898, a campaign was launched to preserve the home as a monument to Betsy Ross. Millions of people contributed to the campaign and the home was purchased, restored, and donated to the city in 1937.

The home is two stories high and includes nine rooms (all filled with wonderful artifacts and authentic colonial furnishings) and a courtyard. My kids can't believe how small and cramped the staircase is. "People must have been really short back then," John says.

Lost Highways Archive and Research Library

307 Market St. 2nd Floor
Philadelphia, PA 19106
(215) 925-2568

Todd Kimmell (who calls himself a "curator/junk man") and his wife Kristin run this unique (some might call it a little eccentric) museum/gallery. This place will be a favorite Philly attraction for auto enthusiasts, especially if you're into vintage stuff (the emphasis is on the period between early 1900s and the 1970s). You'll find an

Lost Highways Archive and Research Library

Hours: By appointment

Directions: From City Hall, take Market east to Third Street.

eclectic mix of info, artifacts and memorabilia related to old cars, trailers and motor homes. If you're in the mood to chat, Todd will be happy to entertain you with tales of his days in the Philly punk club scene.

Historic District

Carpenters Hall

320 Chestnut Street
Philadelphia, PA 19106
(215) 925-0167

The meeting place of 1774's First Continental Congress, Carpenters Hall is still owned by the Carpenters Company of Philadelphia.

Carpenters' Hall was constructed in the early 1770s to house the meetings of the Carpenters' Company (a guild that has included master builders, engineers, and architects, and now consists of over 150 members), which had been congregating in private homes since 1724. The first meeting in the Hall was held in 1771, and the building has remained in the Company's possession ever since. The first Continental Congress met here in 1774; French and American spies gathered in Ben Franklin's second floor library in 1775. For many years, the Hall was the biggest rental property available in the area, so many groups used it to hold meetings and other events. Members' names are listed on the walls. I love the historical aspect—it's amazing to think that Washington, Franklin, and many other legendary colonists climbed the same five granite steps to enter the hall. As a former mason, Jack liked the construction models and related items. However, our kids found the whole thing a little too "educational."

New Hall Military Museum

320 Chestnut Street, next to Carpenters' Hall
(215) 597-8974

A twelve minute film on the development of the U.S. Army and Navy may be seen upstairs. This is a very interesting museum dedicated to the history of American military. The first floor focuses on the Marines. Glass-enclosed displays showcase hand grenades, a blunderbuss, swords, and other Marine weaponry/equipment. I got a kick out of the ration list of daily supplies a soldier received in 1777: 1 lb. bread; 1 lb. pork; 1/2 pound peas; 4 ounces of cheese; and 1/2 pint rum.

The museum's second floor focuses on the Army and Navy. There are lots of cool things here, but be sure to check out the "Try Your Hand at Maneuvering for a Sea Battle" exhibit. To play the game, you have two switches, one of which maneuvers a man-of-war's rudder, while the other trims the sails. Not surprisingly, kids—especially video game veterans—are much better at this than adults.

Chapter Two

Fun Facts

- Shortly after the building was completed in 1791, Secretary of War Henry Knox moved his office from Carpenters' Hall to New Hall.

- During renovations in the 1950s, several artifacts were dug from a cistern about ten feet south of New Hall. The most curious is a brass pipe-tamper.

- The Carpenters' Company met here from 1791 to 1857. After that they met at Carpenters' Hall again.

- "Leatherneck," the nickname for a marine, comes from the leather starks or collars the Marines wore during the Revolution.

The Pretzel Museum

211 North Third Street
Philadelphia, PA 19106
(215) 413-3010

The Pretzel Museum

Hours: Mon-Fri, 8:30 am-5 pm

Ages: 1 and up

Cost: Free

Tours leave from the lobby every fifteen minutes, starting at 10:00 a.m. and running throughout the day. A short film details the history and baking techniques of the pretzel, and there is a table where visitors are given hands-on instructions on the art of pretzel twisting. The museum also contains an on-site pretzel bakery and (this is Brandon's favorite part) all visitors are given a free pretzel at the end of their visit!

Fireman's Hall

147-49 North 2nd Street
Philadelphia, PA 19106
(215) 923-1438

Fireman's Hall

Hours: Tues-Sat, 9 am-5 pm

Cost: Free. Donations accepted.

Directions: From the Visitor Center, take Third Street four blocks north, then turn east on Race.

Formerly the headquarters of Engine Company #8, Fireman's Hall was built at the turn of the century and was an active firehouse from 1902 to 1952. Life-sized figures manning authentic equipment give you a good idea of what life as a firefighter was like during that period. The stained glass and historic/educational displays—such as an authentic 1815 hand pumper and the re-created firemen's living quarters—are wonderful. Kids of all ages seem to love fire trucks and equipment, and this would be especially fascinating to firefighters, EMTs, or other rescue personnel.

Historic District

Elfreth's Alley Museum

126 Elfreth's Alley
Philadelphia, PA 19106
(215) 574-0560
www.elfrethsalley.org

Elfreth's Alley Museum

Hours: Feb-Dec—Tues-Sat, 10 am-4 pm;
Sun, noon-4 pm; Jan—weekends only.
Sat, 10 am-4 pm; Sun, noon-4 pm

Ages: 5 and up

Cost: Adults $2; Children (5-18) $1

Directions: From the Visitor Center, take
Third Street four blocks north and then
turn east on Race.

Elfreth's Alley is the oldest, continuously occupied street in the United States and is lined with charming, quaint houses. You will be transformed back in time to colonial days as you stroll down the cobblestone street, jump over old-time drainage ditches, and lean against hitching posts. Most of the houses are still occupied as private residences (so please be considerate of the people and their homes). I think these residents have the perfect blend of both worlds—old-time living in the midst of the best that modern-day life has to offer. At one end of the street is the small museum, open year-round and features guided tours, a small gift shop, and a garden.

Edward Savaria Jr/ Philadelphia Convention & Visitors Bureau

Chapter Two

Congress Hall

6th and Chestnut Streets
Philadelphia, PA 19106
(215) 597-8974
www.nps.gov/inde/congress-hall.html

Congress Hall

Hours: Daily, 9 am-5 pm;
Closed Christmas and
New Year's Day

Ages: 8 and up

Cost: Free

Directions: Across from
the Liberty Bell on
Chestnut

Congress Hall, as the name suggests, was the home of the U.S. Congress back when Philadelphia was the U.S. Capitol (1790 to 1800, for those of us to whom U.S. history is a bit of a blur). On the first floor in the House chambers, the valances of dark green above the windows enhance the mahogany of the desks and studded leather chairs. In the south bay, there is an alcove where Representatives smoked and drank sherry. Check out the small boxes filled with sand near the fireplaces. These were spitting boxes, used in an age when snuff and chewing tobacco were common. Upstairs, twenty-eight of the thirty-two chairs and the Secretary's desk are authentic. Also remarkable is a nineteenth century fresco of an eagle holding an olive branch, signifying peace. I love the plaster medallion on the ceiling: it has an oval sunburst design honoring the thirteen original states with thirteen stars. The carpet is a reproduction of the original carpet made in the early 1790s by William Sprague of Philadelphia. Its designs are typical patriotic symbols with the centerpiece being a chain of thirteen state shields. In the corners are cornucopias echoing the wish for abundance in the new land. After Congress departed for Washington, D.C., the Hall reverted back to the Philadelphia County Courthouse, the purpose it was built for.

Fun Facts

- George Washington was inaugurated here for his second term.
- John Adams was inaugurated here.
- Vermont, Kentucky, and Tennessee were admitted to Union while Congress sat here.

Historic District

Old City Hall
5th and Chestnut Streets

Standing in front of the Liberty Bell, you'll see Independence Hall flanked by Old City Hall on the left and Congress Hall on the right. Old City Hall was Philadelphia's second city hall and served as the home of the United States Supreme Court between the years of 1791 and 1800.

Philadelphia's original City Hall, built during Penn's lifetime, was near the Delaware River on Second Street. A jail was located downstairs, and upstairs were the Mayor's office and the Mayor's court. Double stairs led to a balcony on the second floor. Voters handed in their ballots on the balcony. The building that served as the city's second City Hall (today known as Old City Hall) was completed in 1791. No sooner had it opened then the municipal government moved in. Upstairs was the Mayor's office and the Mayor's Council Chamber. Downstairs was the Mayor's Court.

Fun Facts

- Old City Hall was the home of the Supreme Court of the United States from 1791 to 1800.

- It was the volunteer headquarters in the battle against Yellow Fever epidemic of 1793.

- Thousands of immigrants entered the U.S. through Philadelphia in the last decade of the eighteenth century. Naturalization ceremonies for new citizens took place in this courtroom.

- In the Second Bank portrait gallery, you can see portraits of five of the Supreme Court Justices who served in Old City Hall: John Jay, Oliver Ellsworth, William Cushing, Samuel Chase, and Bushrod Washington. Also in the Second Bank, you can see a very large painting of Philadelphia's first City Hall (the one that used to stand on 2nd Street).

National Constitution Center

111 S. Independence Mall East
www.constitutioncenter.org

A new attraction scheduled to open July 4, 2003, featuring interactive exhibits, movie theater, and programming that brings to life the U.S. Constitution and how it affects our everyday lives.

Arden Children's Theatre

40 N. 2nd Street
Philadelphia, PA 19106
(215) 922-1122
www.ardentheatre.org

Arden Children's Theatre is Philadelphia's first resident professional children's theatre program, producing children's shows with the same caliber of actors and designers (and budgets) it uses on the main stage.

> **Arden Children's Theatre**
>
> Hours: Box Office—
> Mon-Sat 10 am-6 pm
>
> Directions: From the Visitor Center, take Third two blocks north.

Historic District

Painted Bride Arts Center

230 Vine Street
Philadelphia, PA 19106
(215) 925-9914
www.paintedbride.org

A hotbed of progressive theater, film, music, and dance for all ages, the Painted Bride boasts a comprehensive event calendar. However, it is still a unique place to see quality modern art offerings for the children.

> **Painted Bride Arts Center**
>
> Hours: Tues-Fri, 10 am-6 pm;
> Sat, 12 pm-6 pm
>
> Cost: $8-$25
>
> Directions: From Visitor Center, take Third five blocks north, near the Ben Franklin Bridge

Atwater Kent Museum

15 South Seventh Street
Philadelphia, PA 19106
(215) 685-4832
www.philadelphiahistory.org

You can check out the wampum belt received by William Penn from the Lenni Lenape at Shakamaxon in 1682, furniture used by George Washington during his Presidency in the 1790s, and personal items from Benjamin Franklin. For the sports fan in the family— Phillies' Mike Schmidt's game-worn jersey.

> **Atwater Kent Museum**
>
> Hours: Mon and Wed-Sun, 10 am-5 pm;
> Closed Tuesdays
>
> Ages: 6 and up
>
> Cost: Adults $3;
> Children (3-12) $1.50
>
> Directions: Across from the Liberty Bell on Seventh

Curtis Center

601 Walnut Street
Philadelphia, PA 19106
(215) 238-6484

After leaving the Atwater Kent Museum, take a quick peek in the lobby of the Curtis Center. The glass mosaic called the Dream Garden, and designed by Tiffany, is breathtaking.

> **Curtis Center**
>
> Hours: Mon-Fri, 7 am-6 pm;
> Sat, 10 am-1 pm
>
> Cost: Free

Chapter Two

Three Bears Park

Between 3rd and 4th Streets near Spruce

This tiny playground is geared to the younger set of infants to toddlers. Bits of grass and concrete provide varying running surfaces for toddlers who need to go! There are a couple of benches around the perimeter, but these are a hot commodity, so grab one when you can, or bring your own blanket!

Three Bears Park
Hours: Daily, dawn to dusk
Cost: Free
Directions: From Independence Park, take Fourth Street south two blocks

National Liberty Museum

321 Chestnut Street
Philadelphia, PA 19106
(215) 925-2800
www.libertymuseum.org

This museum's mission is to educate visitors about the country's growing problem of violence and bigotry through a celebration of our country's diversity and freedom. A good lesson for people of all ages. In the **Heroes from Around the World** gallery, I love the replica of Anne Frank's secret annex. From **Conflict to Harmony** features "Jellybean Children" that kids usually think are cool. The three-story tribute to the heroes of 9/11 is very moving.

National Liberty Museum
Hours: Tues-Sun, 10 am-5 pm
Ages: 5 and up
Cost: Adults $5; Seniors $4; Students $3

Declaration House

7th and Market Streets
(215) 597-8780
www.nps.gov/inde/declaration-house.html

Thomas Jefferson rented the two second-floor rooms and drafted the Declaration of Independence here. The house was originally built in 1775 and was reconstructed in 1975. The first floor contains exhibits and a short film on the drafting of the Declaration. On the second floor, the bedroom and parlor that Jefferson occupied have been re-created and contain period piece furnishings. Also included are reproductions of Jefferson's swivel chair and the lap desk he used when he wrote the Declaration.

Declaration House
Hours: Jun-Oct—Daily, 9 am-5 pm; Nov-May—Wed-Sun, 9 am-5 pm
Ages: 7 and up
Cost: Free
Directions: From the Liberty Bell, take Market one block west

Historic District

African-American Museum

701 Arch Street
Philadelphia, PA 19106
(215) 574-0380
www.aampmuseum.org

Edward Savaria Jr/ Philadelphia Convention & Visitors Bureau

African-American Museum

Hours: Tues-Sat, 10 am-5 pm;
Sun 12 pm-5 pm

Cost: Adults $6; Children $4

Directions: From the Liberty
Bell, take Fifth two blocks
north to Arch, then go two
blocks west

Founded in 1976, in celebration of the U.S. Bicentennial, the African American Museum in Philadelphia is dedicated to collecting, preserving, and interpreting the material and intellectual culture of African Americans in Philadelphia. I think the exhibit on slavery is pretty powerful, while my kids find the section devoted to African American sports stars to be more interesting.

Fun Facts

- The Museum hosts an annual all-night jazz jam every February. Jazz legends who have participated in the Jazz 'Til Sunrise show include Shirley Scott, Jimmy Heath, Jimmy Oliver, and Ted Curson.

- The land on which the museum was built was once part of a historic black community.

Mother Bethel A.M.E. Church

419 S. Sixth Street
Philadelphia, PA 19106
(215) 925-0616

Mother Bethel A.M.E. Church

Hours: Call in advance for tour, by appointment only.

Directions: From INHP, take Sixth four blocks south.

First church on site: 1794

Present church built: 1889-1890

The African Methodist Episcopal Church (AME), which today numbers over 2.5 million members, was born in 1777 when a Methodist preacher traveled the Delaware woods, spreading the gospel to a group of slaves, among whom was a seventeen-year-old field hand named Richard Allen. Enslaved and recently separated from several members in his family, who were "sold down the river"—Allen took solace in his belief that he would never be cut off from God's love. The faith that took root in the forest that day would ultimately enable Allen to establish the first A.M.E. Church, Mother Bethel.

Jim McWilliams/ Philadelphia Convention & Visitors Bureau

Historic District

Don't miss the church's stained glass windows. First installed when the church was erected in 1890, they were produced by the Century Art Company at a cost of $1,190. The five windows on the church's Pine Street side depict Biblical references. The windows on the Richard Allen Avenue side are devoted to Jesus Christ. On the Lombard Street side, one of the windows makes significant use of Masonic symbols and was indeed donated by a Masonic order. On the lower level of Mother Bethel is an inspirational three-room museum.

Fun Facts

- Mother Bethel Church was a stop on the Underground Railroad.
- AME is the second-oldest black congregation (after St. Thomas's in Philadelphia) in the country.
- The ground on which Mother Bethel stands is the oldest parcel of real estate continuously owned by African Americans in the United States.
- The second Prince Hall Masonic Lodge was founded here.

Christ Church

20 N. American Street
Philadelphia, PA 19106
(215) 922-1695

Christ Church

Hours: Mon-Sat, 9 am-5 pm; Sun, 12:30 pm-5 pm for guided tours; except in Jan & Feb when it is closed on Mon and Tues. Open for services.

Directions: Located at the corner of Second and Market streets, about two blocks east of the Liberty Bell

At 196 feet high, the church's steeple is a visible landmark from many parts of the city.

Another remarkable feature of the church is the wine glass pulpit built in 1769 by Jon Folwell (who also crafted the Rising Sun chair at Independence Hall). Bishop White preached from this pulpit for fifty-seven years. George Washington and his family attended services sitting in Pew 56, while Pew 70 was reserved for Benjamin Franklin. The box pews were all rented; the balconies were rented with a few free pews left for servants and slaves of parishioners. On July 4, 1788, bells tolled all day to celebrate the ratification of the Constitution.

Fun Facts

- Here you can visit the font in which William Penn was baptized.
- Pew 70 was Ben Franklin's; Washington sat in Pew 56.
- The Second Continental Congress worshipped here as a body in 1775-76.
- Benjamin Franklin organized three lotteries to finance the payment of the church's steeple and bells.

Christt Church Burial Ground
5th St. and Arch
(215) 922-1695

Christ Church Burial Ground is owned by Christ Church and is closed to the public to protect the graves from vandalism. To explore the Burial Ground, you will need to call ahead to Christ Church.

Interred at Christ Church Burial Ground are hundreds of Colonial, Revolutionary and Post-Revolutionary notables, the most famous of whom is Benjamin Franklin. Buried with Franklin is his wife, Deborah, and nearby is a tiny marker for Francis Franklin who died of small pox at age four. After the boy's death, his grieving father urged Philadelphians to inoculate their children against this dreaded disease. Numerous other prominent Philadelphians are buried here.

Fun Facts
- **Five Signers of the Declaration of Independence are buried here.**
- **Visit the Second Bank and Portrait Gallery to see portraits of Benjamin Rush, Francis Hopkinson, James Biddle, William Jackson, and statues of Benjamin Franklin.**
- **The earliest tombstone dates from 1720.**

Historic District

The First Bank of the United States

Third Street, between Chestnut and Walnut Streets

The First Bank of the United States

Directions: Across the street from the Visitor Center

This bank was needed because the government had a debt from the Revolutionary War, and each state had a different form of currency. It was built while Philadelphia was still the nation's capital. Alexander Hamilton conceived of the bank to handle the colossal war debt and to create a standard form of currency. To my kids' disappointment, the bank doesn't give away money as souvenirs. In fact, it's usually closed to the public. But architecturally, it's an interesting place to see.

Fun Facts

- Oldest bank building in America.

- Considered the oldest building in America with a classical façade.

- Bank charter was in effect for only 20 years.

- It cost $110,168.05 to build!

Second Bank of the United States

420 Chestnut Street
Philadelphia, PA 19106
(215) 597-8974

Second Bank of the United States

Hours: Tues-Sun, 10 am-3 pm

Cost: $2.00 for persons 17 and older.

Today the bank is home to the extraordinary Portrait Gallery. Inside the barrel-vaulted structure, graceful Ionic columns compliment the portraits of revolutionary heroes and Federal statesman. Those painted represent a Who's Who of the eighteenth century. There are signers of the Declaration and Constitution in addition to military men and foreign emissaries. Many of the works were painted by Charles Wilson Peale, the foremost portraitist of his day. Other artists include James Sharples and Thomas Sully. Watch for the paintings of Patrick Henry, Casimir Pulaski, and Robert Morris. Oh, kids usually think George Washington's "death mask" is cool.

Chapter Two

Places to Eat

Gianfranco Pizza Rustica

6 N. Third St.
Philadelphia, PA 19106
(215) 592-0048

Gianfranco Pizza Rustica

Hours: Mon-Thurs, 10 am–10 pm;
Fri & Sat, 11 am-11 pm;
Closed Sun

At Gianfranco's you can enjoy a slice of, as Jack says, "real Philly-style pizza." Thin, crispy crust and lots of essential ingredients (chunks of tomato, fresh oregano, and hot bubbling cheese on top) help the pizza earn a thumbs-up from locals who insist on an "authentic" pizza-making approach. The pizza (along with other pizzeria staples like calzone and stromboli) is a hot item (no pun intended) around here; so you may have a little bit of a wait, but your patience will pay off. On a tight budget? The Gianfranco boys "got your back" (as locals would say). They take care of you with a lunch special (two slices and a medium drink for $3.20 from 11:30a.m. to 3:00p.m.). I've heard a few people say that the pizza varies depending on the day and who actually makes it, but it's always been good whenever we've visited. I always get plain slices, but if you want something different, try the veggie style or pizza with roasted peppers and onions.

Historic District

City Tavern

138 South 2nd Street
Philadelphia, PA 19106
(215) 413-1443
www.citytavern.com

The current tavern—built in 1976, just in time for the city's Bicentennial Celebration—is a reconstruction of the tavern originally erected on the site in 1772, and used as a gathering place by delegates to the first and second Continental Congress.

Nick likes the Cornmeal Crusted Chicken Tenders, while John's a fan of the Meat and Cheese Pie. Brandon will happily devour any of the delicious pastries made daily in the on-site bakery.

City Tavern
Hours: Mon-Thurs, 11:30 am-9 pm; Sat 11:30 am-10 pm; Sun 11:30 pm-8 pm
Ages: 5 and up
Cost: Moderate to expensive. Children's menu
Directions: Behind the Visitor Center on Second

Edward Savaria Jr/ Philadelphia Convention & Visitors Bureau

Fun Facts

- John Adams and Thomas Jefferson often met here to enjoy "a feast of reason and a flow of soul."

- Newspapers from the world over were once sold here.

- The dining room was a favorite haunt of Benjamin Franklin.

Willie & Duffy's Philly Grill

620 Chestnut Street
Philadelphia, PA 19106
(215) 413-1744
www.eatacheesesteak.com

Located right next to Independence Hall, Willie & Duffy's offer lots of good eats for breakfast, lunch or dinner. I liked the fast and friendly service (no tipping!).

John likes the Philly Cheese Cake and smoothie drinks, and all the kids enjoyed the cheesesteaks and fries.

Sonny's Famous Steaks

216 Market St.
Philadelphia, PA 19106
(215) 629-4820

Along with cheesesteaks, there are also burgers and fries, chicken fingers, mozzarella sticks, and other lunch favorites. The pizza steaks are about a dollar more than the beef or chicken steaks. You can get Cheez Whiz on top if you really want to indulge.

Historic District

Society Hill

Society Hill runs from the Delaware River to Washington Square and from Walnut Street to Lombard Street. The charm of Society Hill is that its homes are not museums, but are lived in by Philadelphians who delight in eighteenth and nineteenth century houses. As private residences, many of the homes are not open to the public. But there are some you can tour, and you'll also enjoy exploring the hidden paths, cobblestone streets, parks, and trinity houses (three-story, three-room homes).

One of the aspects I find most interesting about Society Hill is the variety of styles and price levels of the homes. You can picture upper-class families mingling side-by-side with their less affluent neighbors.

While there are many beautiful homes and interesting sights in the Society Hill area, I'm not going to devote a huge amount of time to this area, simply because it may be a little too quiet and uneventful to captivate your little ones' attention for very long. If your children are in the older range—or if you've been blessed with little ones with extraordinary long attention spans—there are some interesting places you should try to see.

Headhouse Square
2nd and Pine Streets

Right in the center of Society Hill, Headhouse Square is a historic marketplace complete with a cobblestone street and park.

> **Headhouse Square**
>
> Hours: Open daily, dawn to dusk

Chapter Two

Old St. Joseph's Church

321 Willings Alley
Philadelphia, PA 19106
(215) 923-1733

> **Old St. Joseph's Church**
>
> Directions: From INHP, take
> Second Street two blocks south

Founded in 1733, it is the oldest Roman Catholic church in the city. The entrance to the church is from intimate Willings Alley just off 4th Street. Going through an archway with iron gates, one recalls the legend that Benjamin Franklin advised the Catholic congregation to design the narrow entryway so that, if religious toleration in Philadelphia ever ran a little thin, the church would not be so open to attack. The first church was built in 1733, enlarged in 1821, and rebuilt (the present building) in 1838.

The archway leads to an inner courtyard, with the rectory and its beautifully balanced fascade on the right. A quiet spot, it provides a fitting entry into the church. On the north wall there is a commemorative plaque paying tribute to William Penn, who brought religious toleration and understanding to the colony.

Philadelphia Vietnam Veterans Memorial

Front Street, between Spruce and Delancey

Inspired by her big sister in Washington, D.C., the Philadelphia Vietnam Veterans Memorial honors the memory of the 643 local residents who fell victim in the Vietnam War. The monument lists the names of the fallen warriors engraved in polished marble. Visitors can often be seen etching the names onto pieces of paper—a very touching sight.

> **Philadelphia Vietnam Veterans Memorial**
>
> Directions: From Visitor Center, take Second Street three blocks south

Historic District

Physick House

321 S. Fourth Street
Philadelphia, PA 19106

Physick House

Directions: From INHP,
take Fourth Street four
blocks south

This beautiful home with twenty-two rooms is the only freestanding house in Society Hill. It features an elegantly restored interior, fine Federal and Empire furniture, and a beautiful garden. The house was built in 1786 by Henry Hill, the executor of Benjamin Franklin's will, and was purchased for Dr. Philip Syng Physick by his sister in 1790. The Society of Cincinnatus has its headquarters in the upstairs parlor. A room honoring Dr. Physick and his many surgical inventions is also on the second floor. Antique buffs will want to make sure and see the bedroom, which features a spectacular bed and several fine Chippendale pieces.

Shippen-Wistar House

South Fourth Street

One of the most historically important buildings in Philadelphia is the Shippen-Wistar House, built about 1750 by Dr. William Shippen, a prominent physician who served in the Continental Congress in 1778 and 1779. It was then occupied by Dr. William Shippen, Jr. One of the first to use bodies for dissection, he faced accusations of "body snatching." Richard Henry Lee, Francis Lightfoot Lee, George Washington and John Adams were among the guests known to have visited here.

Chapter Two

A Man Full of Trouble

125-127 Spruce Street
Philadelphia, PA 19106

This is the only tavern remaining from Colonial Philadelphia. It was built about 1759 on the banks of Little Dock Creek (long since filled in and lost to view), in an area in which mariners and dockhands patronized this inn.

With its low ceilings and cozy feel, the tavern is warm and inviting. Superb English Delft china, old pewter, and a set of Windsor chairs owned by the first Chief Justice, John Jay, are all on view. Pipe smokers dropped money in an "Honesty Box," which demanded a penny and then the honesty of the pipe smoker who would take only one pipeful of tobacco.

> **A Man Full of Trouble**
>
> Directions: From Visitor Center, go south on Third Street three blocks, then turn onto Spruce.

American Street

Between Second and Third Street

Off Delancey Street, between Second and Third, take a stroll on American Street. You'll see small houses with their appealing pent eaves above the first floor, a formal Japanese garden adjacent to an eighteenth century house, and Drinker's Court (1765)—a tiny and charming hideaway.

Cadwalader House

Fourth Street

Built in 1826 by Joseph Parker Norris in what had been a garden of the Shippen-Wistar House, this four-story house (plus dormered attic) has particularly graceful fanlights over both doors that face 4th Street. It was bought in 1837 by Judge John Cadwalader.

> **Cadwalader House**
>
> Directions: Adjoining the Shippen-Wistar House at 240 South 4th Street, and abutting the burial ground of St. Mary's Church.

Historic District

Old St. Mary's Church

252 S. Fourth Street
Philadelphia, PA 19106

Old St. Mary's Church
Directions: Fourth Street, three blocks south of INHP

Founded in 1763, this was the first Roman Catholic cathedral of the Diocese of Philadelphia and was enlarged in 1810 and renovated in 1963. Although St. Joseph's Church was founded first, the present building of St. Mary's is older than that of St. Joseph's. Washington, who apparently showed no favoritism when it came to attending services, worshipped here as well as at Christ Church and St. Peter's.

Along the north wall of its burial ground are found the graves of the early Bouviers. Jacqueline Kennedy Onassis's great-great grandfather Michel Bouvier, the first of the family to come from France, and his descendants all lie beneath the vault. Thomas FitzSimons, signer of the Constitution, member of the Continental Congress and Representative in the first three Congresses of the United States; and Stephen Moylan, a general officer in the Revolution and aide-de-camp to Washington, both all lie in this old and historic burial ground. Here, too, is the grave of Commodore John Barry, "Father of the American Navy."

Powel House

244 S. Third Street
Philadelphia, PA 19106

Powel House
Directions: Three blocks south of Visitor Center

Said to be one of the finest Georgian houses in the United States, the Powel House was built in 1765 and purchased in 1768 by Samuel Powel, the last Colonial mayor of Philadelphia and the first mayor after the Revolution. Samuel's wife, Elizabeth, was a sister of Thomas Willing, who with his partner Robert Morris helped finance the Revolution. Powel, like so many other Philadelphians, died of the yellow fever in 1793, but the family remained in the house for over forty years. The second-floor ballroom with its magnificent Waterford chandelier contains a pianoforte from 1795, as well as a French harp and an arm harp.

Franklin Square

Northeast Square, as it was originally called, is the least known of the city's squares. In the eighteenth century, part of the square was used as a burial ground, and some graves remain today, covered over by the lawns and grass. After the Vine Street Expressway and Ben Franklin Bridge were added nearby, the square became more isolated and forgotten, even though it is pretty close to the heavily populated Independence Park area. The square features a pool, playground equipment, a small baseball diamond, and plenty of benches, so it's worth visiting if you don't mind the heavy traffic surrounding the place. Be sure to look for the memorial to the Philadelphia police and firefighters killed in the line of duty. From the square's east side, you get a nice view of the Bolt of Lightning, a memorial to Ben Franklin. Located across Sixth Street in Monument Plaza, the huge sculpture depicts Franklin's famous "kite and key" experiment.

Penn's Landing

As the name suggests, this is the area where William Penn, Philadelphia's founder, first touched ground in his "greene country towne," as he called it. Penn's Landing stretches along the Delaware River for about ten blocks from Vine Street to South Street. After Penn's arrival, this area quickly became the center of Philly's maritime soul and the city's dominant commercial district. Today, however, Penn's Landing is a riverside park and the place where Philadelphians gather, in the summer to hear music and on December 31 to usher in the New Year.

Blue Cross River Rink

121 N Columbus Blvd
(215) 925.7465
www.riverrink.com

A great place for ice skating and just enjoying the crisp winter air, River Rink opens toward the end of November and stays open through February. Recently began offering sled

Blue Cross River Rink
Hours: Nov-Feb, Mon-Thurs, 6 pm-9 pm; Fri-Sat, 12:30 pm-10:30 pm; Sun 12:30 pm-9 pm
Cost: $5-$6; skate rental: $3

skating specifically designed for kids and adults with disabilities. A fun game: see how many orange Philadelphia Flyers jerseys you can spot in the area!

Historic District

Independence Seaport Museum

211 South Columbus Blvd
(215) 925-5439
www.phillyseaport.org

Independence Seaport Museum

Hours: Daily, 10 am-5 pm

Cost: Adults $8; Children (5-12) $4; Seniors $6.50

Directions: From the Visitors Center on 3rd Street just south of Chestnut Street, it's an easy five-block walk to the Museum. Walk a half block south to Walnut Street, turn left to 2nd Street and past Olde Original Bookbinder's Restaurant to Front Street, then straight ahead over the pedestrian bridge crossing highway I-95. You will see the Delaware River ahead and the Museum on your right as you walk down the steps (there is an elevator if needed). Stop # 12 on the PHLASH route.

All kids (especially boys) seem to love ships, so this is a very popular family attraction. Check out the **What Floats Your Boat** interactive exhibit, where you can test boat models in water and wind, plank a wooden boat, and put together a boat frame. In the **Coming to America** exhibit, kids can climb into gray bunks like the ones immigrants would have been crammed into while riding in steerage compartments—your kids might just realize how good they have it at home when compared to this!

Rusty Kennedy/ Philadelphia Convention & Visitors Bureau

Tip
To avoid the crowds, it's best to visit on a weekday afternoon or weekend morning.

Chapter Two

Olympia World War I Cruiser and Becuna World War II Submarine

Penn's Landing Columbus Blvd.

The Cruiser OLYMPIA (C-6) is the last surviving veteran of the Spanish-American War of 1898, and the oldest steel warship afloat in the world. Launched in January 1944 during the height of World War II, Submarine BECUNA (SS-319) completed five wartime patrols in the Pacific Ocean.

> **Olympia World War I Cruiser and Becuna World War II Submarine**
>
> Hours: Daily 10am-5pm
>
> Cost: included with admission to Seaport Museum.

Spirit of Philadelphia

The Philadelphia Marine Center, the Piers at Penn's Landing
(215) 923-1419

Dinner cruise on the Delaware River.

A nice relaxing way to see the area and relax after a hard day of sightseeing (or shopping). Don't worry about getting seasick—the Delaware River is generally very calm, and you can hardly tell the ship is moving. The night cruises tend to be on the formal side; but for lunch cruises, casual dress is fine. In addition to dance music, the cruises feature some great entertainers (singers, comedians, etc.).

> **Spirit of Philadelphia**
>
> Hours: Lunch, Mon-Fri, noon-2 pm; Dinner, Mon-Sat, 7 pm-10 pm; Sun, 12:30 pm-2:30 pm

RiverLink Ferry

Penn's Landing, Columbus Blvd.
(215) 925-LINK
www.riverlinkferry.org

The RiverLink Ferry operates seven days a week from April 1st through November 18th, with departures every twenty minutes from either Philadelphia or the New Jersey State Aquarium. During special waterfront events, the ferry operates extended hours.

> **RiverLink Ferry**
>
> Hours: Apr 1-Nov 18—Daily, 9:40 am-5:40 pm. Departures every 40 min.
>
> Cost: Round-trip—Adults $5; Children $3

Historic District

Moshulu Sailing Ship Restaurant

Penn's Landing, Columbus Blvd.
(215) 923-2500

Fully restored nineteenth-century sailing ship, and features fine dining.

> **Moshulu Sailing Ship Restaurant**
> Hours: Daily, 11:30 am-midnight

The world's largest and oldest four-masted sailing ship, the Moshulu was moved in May 2002 from its previous location and now sits between the Olympia and the Spirit of Philadelphia.

Fun Fact

The Moshulu has appeared in numerous films, including *Rocky* and *The Godfather*.

International Sculpture Garden

Penn's Landing
Philadelphia, PA 19106
(215) 546-7550

Located on Columbus Boulevard between Chestnut and Spruce Streets, the International Sculpture Garden features lots of sculptures from many different cultures and time periods. I like the Spheres from Costa Rica, and the House Post Totem Pole. My kids think the Elephant Water Spout sculpture is pretty cool, too.

Dave and Buster's

325 N. Columbus Blvd.
Philadelphia, PA 19106
(215) 413-1951
www.daveandbusters.com

> **Dave and Buster's**
> Hours: Sun-Tues, 11:30 am -midnight;
> Wed-Thurs 11:30 am-1 am;
> Fri-Sat, 11:30 am-2 am
>
> Ages: 10 and up
>
> Cost: Bring cash

Although this is part of a national chain, I'm including it here because too many kids, (including mine) say it's a "must see" Philly attraction. If your kids have squirmed through a few too many historical tours, this is the perfect place for them to let off some pent-up energy while Mom and Dad take a breather and plot out the route for the rest of the day's tour.

Kids will love this place; although it's actually designed for adults. Alcohol is served, and the place can get thick with cigarette smoke in spots. As long as you keep a close eye on your kids, though, you'll have fun. In fact, they'll have such a good time, it'll be a challenge to get them out of the place. In addition to the usual arcade fare, there are lots of high-tech interactive and virtual reality games. Forget about claiming to have run out of quarters—that ruse will no longer work, thanks to the oh-so-helpful (yeah right) D&B automatic swipe card that lets you recharge it almost as fast as your kids can spend it.

Chapter Two

Ben Franklin Bridge

In order to get from Philadelphia to Camden, New Jersey, you cross the Delaware River by taking the Ben Franklin Bridge. If you're driving, be sure to have cash, as it costs a couple of dollars to cross the bridge. If you're walking, make sure you have lots of energy; it's almost two miles across one-way. At night, you can spot the bridge from miles away, thanks to the cool lighting effects.

Northeast Philadelphia/Northern Liberties

This is the area north of Vine St. and east towards the river. This is a rough area and industrial; although an effort is currently underway to try and revive the area to make it more tourist-friendly. Although this area is becoming more popular among the adult crowd, it's not really family-oriented, and really the only site of interest is the St. John Neumann Shrine (although if you have teenagers, they may try to convince you that the popular Electric Factory Concert venue qualifies as a "tourist attraction").

St. John Neumann Shrine

1019 N. 5th St.
Philadelphia, PA 19123
(215) 627-3080
www.stjohnneumann.org

Located about a mile north of Independence Hall, the most fascinating thing about this shrine is that St. John Neumann's remains are buried under the altar. The shrine features a museum and gift shop.

> **St. John Neumann Shrine**
>
> Hours: Mon-Sat, 7:30 am-6:00 pm;
> Sun, 7:30 am-5:00 pm
>
> Directions: From Independence
> Park, take Fifth Street north
> about a mile.

Chapter Three

Center City

Although we often wind up visiting Center City on the weekends because of our hectic school/work schedules; I definitely prefer weekday visits if at all possible. For one thing, you can only tour the City Hall tower on weekdays. Also, two of our other favorite nearby hotspots—the Masonic Temple and the Reading Terminal Market—are closed on Sundays. Sure, the traffic (both the pedestrian and motorized kind) is much heavier during the week, but experiencing the hustle and bustle of busy city life is actually one of my favorite parts. If you want to avoid crowds—or if you'd feel more comfortable walking around with your kids in the area—then a weekend visit may be the better choice for you.

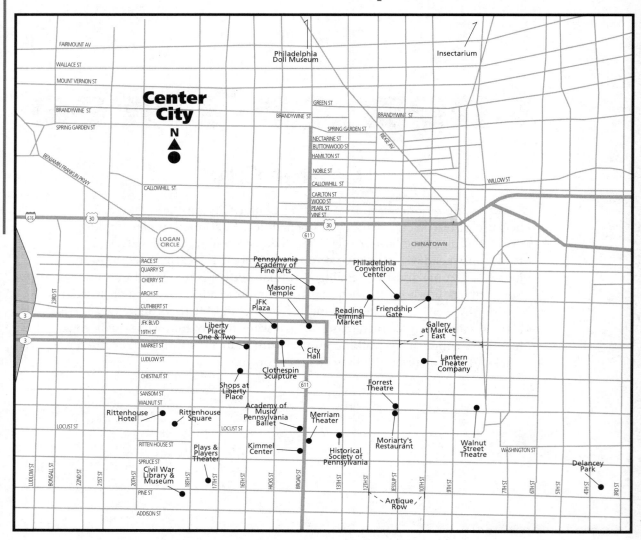

Center City

The City Hall Area

City Hall

Broad and Market Streets
Philadelphia, PA 19107
(215) 686-1776

City Hall

Hours: Tower Mon-Fri
9:30 am-4:30 pm;
Tours Mon-Fri 12:30 pm

Cost: Free

Edward Savaria Jr./Philadelphia Convention & Visitors Bureau

You can't miss City Hall. For one thing, it's a massive building smack dab in the middle of the city. Plus, the huge statue of William Penn atop City Hall is hard to overlook (although for some reason, many people assume the statue is one of Ben Franklin). At one time, there was an informal agreement that nothing in the city would be taller than the statue's hat. One of the five Philadelphia squares is Penn Square, which is entirely occupied by City Hall.

Chapter Three

Stop at the tour office and pick up a copy of *Philadelphia City Hall Tower Views*, and, if your kids are up to it, take a tour of some of *City Hall's* 700 rooms, including the Mayor's Reception Room, the Supreme Court, and the City Council Meeting room. Take the elevator up to observation deck, and enjoy a great view of the city.

As a former mason, Jack finds City Hall interesting from an architectural standpoint. It's the tallest masonry bearing building in the world—no steel reinforcements support the building.

Hollywood Tidbit

The grounds outside City Hall were used to shoot a scene featuring an AIDS demonstration in the movie *Philadelphia*, and Courtroom 243 was also featured prominently in the movie.

JFK Plaza (also known as the Love Park)

JFK Blvd. and 15th Street

> **JFK Plaza**
> **(also known as the Love Park)**
>
> Directions: From City Hall, take Market Street one block west, and head one block north.

Officially called JFK Plaza, locals generally refer to this area as the "Love Park," in reference to the big Love sculpture found there. The sculpture was created by Robert Indiana and unveiled in 1976 as part of Philadelphia's bicentennial celebration. While the Love statue has become iconic with Philly (which, after all, is known as the "City of Brotherly Love"), my kids are actually much more fond of other pieces of art in the plaza. The park features game pieces (standing several feet high) from the popular board games Monopoly and Sorry, as well as some Domino pieces. Most kids have a ball playing around these big game pieces, and my kids are no different. John gravitates toward the Monopoly pieces, while Nick heads for the dominos and Brandon circles the Sorry pieces.

Although, skateboarding is not allowed at the Plaza and police make a valiant effort to keep the area free of skaters, JFK Plaza is supposedly seen in skateboarding circles as one of the ultimate East Coast destinations. Stone walls, granite pavement, lots of wide, flat benches, steps and railings galore apparently make it a skaters' paradise. City officials tossed around various plans to renovate the park, making it more appealing to pedestrians and the "power lunch" crowd and less appealing to skaters and the rodents that are often spotted in the area. They did recently spruce up the park by adding new trees, wooden benches and better

Center City

lighting. Also, the opening of a demonstration skate park at Thirteenth and Arch Streets is supposed to alleviate some of the skater activity. But it's still a good idea to keep alert and try to stay out of the path of a speeding skater. Speaking of skateboarding, the ESPN X-Games were held in Philly in 2001 and 2002, although Los Angeles will host the games in 2003.

As part of their vision for JFK Plaza, city officials would also like to do something with the nearby Visitors Center, which remains vacant since being replaced by the Independence Visitors Center.

Jim McWilliams/ Philadelphia Convention & Visitors Bureau

Chapter Three

Clothespin Sculpture

15th and Market Street

Clothespin Sculpture

Directions: From City Hall, take Market Street one block west.

Oldenburg's *Clothespin*, a 45-foot high steel sculpture, was controversial at first, but seems to have grown on locals and has now become a Philadelphia icon.

From the *Clothespin*, you can catch the Market-Frankford subway to get to the Insectarium.

Philadelphia Doll Museum

2253 N. Broad Street
Philadelphia, PA 19132
(215) 787-0220
www.philadollmuseum.com

Although, my three boys were totally against going anywhere near something called the "doll museum," I found this place really interesting. The renowned Roberta Bell Doll collection includes African, European, American Folk Art dolls, internationally manufactured dolls and more. There's a special emphasis on the preservation of black dolls as artifacts of history and culture. I really like the folk art collection, featuring "rag dolls" and dolls made from lots of different materials such as bottles, tobacco and cornhusk. The one drawback of the museum is its location. It's fairly far from Center City and most other Philly attractions, and therefore it is in a section of the city that is difficult for tourists who are unfamiliar with the area, to wander around.

Center City

Insectarium

8046 Frankford Avenue
Philadelphia, PA 19136
(215) 338-3000
 www.insectarium.com

Not being a big fan of insects, I personally was shocked that someone would actually devote a museum to these creepy critters, but some people—especially boys—find this place fascinating. There's a million bugs (about one-fourth of them are alive, and the rest are preserved in some manner). You'll find everything from scorpions to centipedes, and of course a bunch of tarantulas thrown in for good measure. You can also buy "bug stuff" at the gift shop.

> **Insectarium**
>
> Directions: Take the Market-Frankford subway from the Clothespin and transfer to SEPTA Bus 66. Or if driving, follow Roosevelt Boulevard (US Route 1 North) to the Cottman Avenue Exit and turn right. Follow Cottman Ave (Route 73) to Frankford Avenue and make a left to 8046 Frankford Avenue. The Insectarium is on the left side between Rhawn Street and Welsh Road.

Masonic Temple

1 N. Broad Street
Philadelphia, PA 19107
(215) 988-1917

Even many locals have never visited the Masonic Temple, and they're really missing out, because it truly is an awesome site. This is another building that indulges Jack's interest in masonry. Built in 1868 by the

> **Masonic Temple**
>
> Free admission
>
> Tours: Mon-Fri 10 am, 11 am, 1 pm, 2 pm and 3 pm; Sat, 10 am and 11 am
>
> Directions: From City Hall, head one block north and cross JFK Blvd.

members of the Free Masons (a group that traces its roots back to the group of stoneworkers in the Middle Ages who supposedly held secret meetings and had special passwords and codes) the temple features seven lodge halls which each exemplify specific styles of architecture. John and Nick, who have done several school project on Egypt, really liked the Egyptian room with its "cool" hieroglyphics. Many prominent men of colonial times were Masons, including many who weren't involved in the building trade at all. The cornerstone of this temple was set in place with the same trowel that George Washington—a member of Masons—has used to set the cornerstone of the U.S. Capitol.

Chapter Three

Liberty Place One and Two

16th and Market Street

One Liberty Place is a sixty-three story building that was the first "skyscraper" in Philly and the first building to exceed the height of the Penn statue at City Hall. Two Liberty Place is home to the Westin Philadelphia hotel.

Liberty Place One and Two
Location: 16th and Market St.

Pennsylvania Academy of Fine Arts

118 N. Broad Street
Philadelphia, PA 19102
(215) 972-7600
www.pafa.org

Located in a beautiful Victorian Gothic building, the PAFA is the country's oldest art school and museum. You can see the works of a wide range of artists, from Edwin Dickinson and Andrew Wyeth to Andy Warhol and Barry Goldberg. However, this destination might be a little too stifling for younger kids or those with a short attention span.

Pennsylvania Academy of Fine Arts
Hours: Tues-Sat, 10 am to 5 pm; Sun, 11 am to 5 pm
Directions: From Masonic Temple, take Broad Street two blocks north
Cost: $5 adults; $4 seniors and students with I.D.; $3 ages 18 and under

Delancey Park

Delancey Street between Third and Fourth Streets

The perfect place for Mom and Dad to take a break while the little ones blow off some steam. Lots of things to climb on, plus fountains to keep everyone cool.

Center City

Where to Shop

Philly actually has two neighborhoods devoted to specific types of shopping—Antique Row and Jewelers' Row. Both are geared toward leisurely shopping and higher-priced items. If you're like me, this type of thing isn't high on your priority list when enjoying some precious vacation time with your kids—plus, my kids would last about five minutes doing some "leisurely shopping" with me before they decided they'd had enough. But should you have some spare time for yourself (while your spouse entertains the kids at the hotel pool, perhaps), I'm including some brief information on these shopping regions.

Antique Row

Pine Street between 9th and 12th Streets

Edward Savaria Jr/ Philadelphia Convention & Visitors Bureau

Accent on Design
1032 Pine St
Philadelphia, PA 19107
(215) 733-0703

Amaradio's Antiques
918 Pine Street
Philadelphia, PA 19107
(215) 238-9482

Antique Design
1102 Pine Street
Philadelphia, PA 19107
(215) 629-1812

Specializing in restored antique stained glass.

Blendo Past and Present
1002 Pine Street
Philadelphia, PA 19107
(215) 351-9260

Chapter Three

Bookline International
1018 Pine Street
Philadelphia, PA 19107
(215) 238-1262

Classic Antiques
922 Pine Street
Philadelphia, PA 19107
(215) 629-0211

Déjà vu Collectibles
1038 Pine Street
Philadelphia, PA 19107
(215) 923-9895

Eloquence Antiques and Decorative Arts
1034 Pine Street
Philadelphia, PA 19107
(215) 627-6606

G.B. Schaffer Antiques
1014 Pine Street
Philadelphia, PA 19107
(215) 923-2263

Hello World
1201 Pine Street
Philadelphia, PA 19107
(215) 545-7060

Jansen Antiques
1042 Pine Street
Philadelphia, PA 19107
(215) 922-5594

Jeffrey Lee Biber (IONIAN) Antiques
1030 Pine Street
Philadelphia, PA 19107
(215) 574-3633

M. Finkle & Daughter
936 Pine Street
Philadelphia, PA 19107
(215) 627-7797

Show of Hands
1006 Pine Street
Philadelphia, PA 19107
(215) 592-4010

Center City

Jewelers' Row

Centered around Samson Street, between 7th and 8th Street, Jewelers' Row encompasses more than 300 retailers and jewelers.

The Gallery at Market East

Market Street from Eighth to Eleventh Street
Philadelphia, PA 19107
(215) 625-4962
www.galleryatmarketeast.com

The Gallery at Market East
Hours: Mon, Tues, Thurs, and Sat 10 am to 7 pm, Wed-Fri 10 am-8 pm, and Sun noon-5 pm
Directions: From INHP, take Market Street three blocks west

A mall that spans four city blocks, The Gallery is a nice place to do some shopping (or seek shelter from inclement weather) while trekking from Old City to Center City. From the fourth floor, you can get a great view of the whole place. My kids love the tall colorful banners, figures and other decorations that "climb" up from the center section near the elevators. Stores include the usual like Old Navy, the Gap and Kmart, as well as some more unusual places like Lids (a hat store), Dr. Denim and the Italian Show Warehouse. There are lots of places to eat, too.

Shops at Liberty Place

1625 Chestnut Street
Philadelphia, PA
(215) 851-9055

Located between Liberty Place One and Two, the Shops at Liberty place is a two-story mall featuring upscale retailers and a second-floor food court offering just about any type of food you could want. My kid's always have to make a wish in the fountain, and we once saw a cool sandcastle competition in the first-floor rotunda.

Chapter Three

Lord & Taylor

1300 Market St.
Philadelphia, PA 19107
(215) 241-9000

Lord & Taylor

Directions: From City Hall, take Market Street east two blocks

This twelve story building features a huge department store, as well as a dry cleaner, beauty salon, and the "Iggle," a huge eagle stature that the locals are pretty fond of. A Christmas sound and light show runs through the holiday season. While shopping, enjoy pipe organ performances throughout the day.

Hollywood Tidbit

The movies *Mannequin and Mannequin Two* were filmed at Lord & Taylor (formerly Wanamaker's). And in *Blow Out*, John Travolta drove his car through Wanamaker's window.

Karl's Juvenile Furniture

724 Chestnut St
Philadelphia, PA 19106
(215) 627-2514

Adorable cribs and Sweet Pea baby furniture, as well as cute infant accessories, clothes for babies and kids up to twelve years old. On weekends, the place tends to be crowded with pregnant women.

Born Yesterday

1901 Walnut St
Philadelphia, PA 19103
(215) 568-6556

Born Yesterday

Directions: Take Walnut Street to 17th Street

Hours: Mon-Sat, 10 am-6 pm

This small children's boutique has unique toys (like plush castles and farmhouses) and stylish kids' clothes.

Electric Factory

421 N. 7th St.
Philadelphia, PA 19123
(215) 568-3222

Electric Factory

Cost: varies

Directions: Take Seventh Street past Route 676 to the intersection of Seventh and Callowhill Street.

Small concert venue, typically rock and pop performers. This would probably interest the teens and pre-teens in the family. Perhaps you can treat them to a concert here to make up for forcing them to sit through a theater production.

Center City

Where to Eat

Spaghetti Warehouse

1026 Spring Garden St.
Philadelphia, PA 19123
(215) 787-0784

Yes, it's part of a national chain, but this is one of our favorite places to eat. Before we ever walked through the door the first time, we knew it would be the perfect place for John, a pasta fanatic. But it's a hit with the whole family, partly because of the great atmosphere. Watch for the mascot, Uncle Skeddy, who likes to clown around with the kids. They have a trolley car that you can sit in while you eat, but it only fits two people. Watch for special family deals on weekends (kids can often eat for 99 cents).

> **Spaghetti Warehouse**
>
> Hours: Sun-Thurs, 11 am-10 pm;
> Fri-Sat, 11 am-11 pm
>
> Directions: Take 11th Street north to Spring Garden Street and make a right.

Bertucci's

1515 Locust Street
Philadelphia, PA 19102
(215) 731-1400

Bertucci's is known for their thin crust pizza baked in a brick oven. Even a plain pie tastes great, but if you feel adventurous, go for something different, like the barbequed chicken pizza.

> **Bertucci's**
>
> Hours: Mon-Thurs, 11 am-10 pm;
> Fri, 11 am-11 pm;
> Sat 11 am-11:30 pm;
> Sun noon-9 pm

Academy Cafe

2nd floor in the Doubletree Hotel, on Broad St. at Locust St.
Philadelphia, PA 19103
(215) 893-1667

An upscale restaurant for great American dining. Try the jumbo shrimp cocktail or the lamb chops. At night, the Academy Café tends to attract an older theater crowd.

> **Academy Cafe**
>
> Directions: From City Hall, take Broad Street two blocks south.

Chapter Three

Moriarty's Restaurant

1116 Walnut Street
Philadelphia, PA 19107
(215) 627-7676

> **Moriarty's Restaurant**
>
> Directions: From Washington Square, take Market Street west four blocks. Located next to the Forrest Theatre.

Features a gaslight mystery theatre. They have good food at reasonable prices. I like the fried mozzarella, but if you're more adventurous, try the Moriarty's Firecrackers (jalapeno peppers stuffed with cream cheese and coated in Italian bread crumbs).

Hard Rock Cafe

1113-31 Market Street
Philadelphia, PA 19107
(215) 238-1000
www.hardrock.com/locations/cafes/Cafes.asp?Lc=PHIL

> **Hard Rock Cafe**
>
> Hours: Sun-Thurs, 11 am-12 pm; Fri-Sat, 11 am-1 am
>
> Cost: Moderate
>
> Directions: Located in the Reading Terminal Market

Although part of a national chain, the Hard Rock in Philly is still kind of unique, since each Hard Rock location features a unique collection of musical memorabilia. There's definitely some impressive stuff here—but what else would you expect in the town that gave us American Bandstand? As with most theme restaurants, the food really isn't the main attraction here (although Jack's pretty fond of the Heavy Metal chicken wings). Frankly, since a lot of the memorabilia is from the "classic rock" age featuring artists like the Rolling Stones, Prince, Elton John and Black Sabbath, much of the enjoyment for kids is just watching their parents act like goofy wide-eyed teenagers as they recall their long-gone "cool" days. My kids usually just roll their eyes and pretend they don't know me as I stare awe-struck at Eddie Van Halen's guitar or the black shirt that Prince once wore onstage during a concert in the 1990s.

Jim McWilliams/ Philadelphia Convention & Visitors Bureau

Center City

Other Attractions of Interest

Rittenhouse Square
Walnut Street, between 18th and 19th Streets

Len Redkoles/ Philadelphia Convention & Visitors Bureau

One of Philadelphia's five squares, Rittenhouse Square is a popular and beautiful park with a fountain, sculptures and lots of benches. And—this is important if you've got kids with you—there are lots of public restrooms available at the nearby stores. Many shows are held at Rittenhouse Square, especially during the warm weather, such as the Rittenhouse Square Fine Arts Annual, an art show held here in June.

The area surrounding Rittenhouse Square is one of Philly's most upscale residential neighborhoods, so this is a very safe part of the city. The nearby shopping area—nicknamed Rittenhouse Row—contains many of Philly's swankest shops and boutiques.

Chapter Three

Civil War Library & Museum

1805 Pine St.
Philadelphia, PA 19107
(215) 735-8196

Feature Civil War uniforms, weapons, artwork, and a 12,000-volume library. Kids usually like the Abraham Lincoln masks, along with the battle swords.

Civil War Library & Museum

Hours: Thurs-Sat,11 am-4:30 pm

Cost: $5 adults, $4 seniors, $3 students, $2 ages 3-12, free under 3

Historical Society of Pennsylvania

1300 Locust St.
Philadelphia, PA
(215) 732-6200 x.412
www.hsp.org

Historical Society of Pennsylvania

Hours: 9:30 am-4 pm, Tues, Thurs, Fri, 1 pm-8 pm, Wed, Sat, 10 am-4 pm

Cost: $6 adults, $3 students

You can find lots of books of books and old manuscripts here, but that probably wouldn't be the kids' idea of a good time. However, this is also one of the country's largest family history resource centers, so tracing your family tree might make a good group project.

Theaters

When it comes to kids and the theater, I've noticed that there seems to be no middle ground—they either love it or hate it. My kids are not the biggest fans of theater, but I know some of their friends love seeing a theater production. Since, Philadelphia has an incredible array of theaters, I wanted to include them here for those of you with young theater buffs in the family. I've included brief information on some of the top theaters in town.

Center City

Kimmel Center for the Performing Arts

260 South Broad Street (Avenue of the Arts)
Suite 901
Philadelphia, PA 19102
(215) 790-5800
www.kimmelcenter.org

Kimmel Center for the
Performing Arts

Directions: From Market
Street, take Broad Street
two blocks south.

   The Kimmel Center has two major venues: Verizon Hall, a 2,500-seat concert hall built specifically as the home of The Philadelphia Orchestra; and Perelman Theater, a 650-seat recital theater that can adapt to a variety of presentations. Box Office is open daily from 10:00 a.m. to 6:00 p.m., or until one-half hour after the last performance begins. The Kimmel frequently hosts ballets like *The Nutcracker*.

Roman Vilony/ Philadelphia Convention & Visitors Bureau

Chapter Three

Plays & Players Theater

1714 Delancey St.
Philadelphia, PA 19102
(215) 985-1400

Plays & Players Theater

Directions: Take 17th Street
south to Delancey Street.

A children's theater with about 320 comfy seats, all of which provide a good view of the stage. Seems to emphasize plays that have some kind of social or moral message.

The Academy of Music/Pennsylvania Ballet

Broad and Locust Streets
Philadelphia, PA 19102
(215) 893-1955
www.academyofmusic.org

**The Academy of
Music/Pennsylvania Ballet**

Hours: Box Office
Mon-Sat 10 am-5:30 pm

Directions: From City Hall,
take Broad Street four
blocks south.

Home to the Pennsylvania Ballet, the Philadelphia Opera, and the Philadelphia Orchestra. The Academy of Music is one of the city's premier cultural institutions.

Hollywood Tidbit

The Academy was used to film the opening scenes of *The Age of Innocence*. Although it was the middle of spring, producers had to close down the street for three days in order to create the "winter wonderland" necessary to shoot the winter scenes.

Merriam Theater

250 South Broad Street
Philadelphia, PA 19102
(215) 732-5446

Merriam Theater

Hours: Box office:
Mon-Sat 10 am-5:30 pm

Cost: $39.50-$62.50

Directions: From Market, take
Broad Street two blocks south.

The home stage for the University of the Arts, the Merriam also plays host to Broadway shows and the PA Ballet. It's been a Philly institution since 1918, when it opened at the Shubert Theater.

Center City

Walnut Street Theatre

825 Walnut Street
Philadelphia, PA 19107
(215) 574-3550 ext. 4
www.wstonline.org

Walnut Street Theatre is the oldest theatre in America. It stands alone as the only theatre operating continuously as a theatre since it opened in 1809.

Lantern Theater Company

10th and Ludlow St.
P.O. Box 53428
Philadelphia, PA 19105
(215) 829-9002
www.lanterntheater.org

Generally shows classical theatrical productions, such as Shakespeare's works.

Forrest Theatre

1114 Walnut Street
Philadelphia, PA 19107
(215) 923-1515
www.forrest-theatre.com

Owned by the Shubert Organization, the Forrest is often called Philly's own "Broadway" theatre. We saw a great production of *Phantom of the Opera* here. Upcoming shows for 2003 include *The Tale of the Allergist's Wife* and *Mamma Mia!*

Tours

76 Carriage Company/Carriage Rides

Philadelphia (citywide), PA
(215) 923-8516
www.phillytour.com

This carriage tour company provides a private, stylish, horse-led coach for neighborhood tours throughout the city.

Chapter Three

Walk Philadelphia:
Guided Tours of the City and Region
Various locations throughout Center City
(215) 440-5500
www.centercityphila.org/tours

There are forty-seven tours in all, twenty-seven throughout Center City Philadelphia. All tours last approximately one to two hours.

> **Walk Philadelphia:**
> **Guided Tours of the City and Region**
>
> Season: Spring - November
>
> Cost: Tour fee of $10/person ($8/person for students, including college students with valid ID - children age 10 and under: FREE and must be accompanied by an adult)

Chinatown Tour
(215) 772-0739

Includes lunch of dinner. Reservations required.

American Trolley Tours
(215) 333-2119

Departs daily from various hotels and the Visitors Center.

Chinatown

This area from 9th to 11th Streets, between Arch and Vine Streets, is home to dozens of Asian restaurants, markets, bakeries and shops.

To find out more about the area, check out www.phillychinatown.com.

My kids love the pagoda-style Oriental phone booths in the neighborhood, and of course if you like Chinese food (as well as Vietnamese, Cambodian, Thai or other Asian cuisine), you've come to the right place.

Friendship Gate
10th & Arch St., Chinatown

This striking forty-foot high metal archway greets you as you enter Chinatown. The gate (the largest authentic type of its kind outside of China) was made by a Chinese craftsman, using materials and tools from their native land.

Center City

Asia Crafts

123 N. 10th St.
Philadelphia, PA 19107
(215) 925-3974

Asia Crafts
Directions: Half a block from the Friendship Gate, next to the Cultural Center.

This store is kind of small, but it'll be a big hit with the girls in your family. Almost everything in the store has the "Hello Kitty" logo—from purses to toys, and even shower curtains!

Trocadero

1003 Arch St.
Philadelphia, PA 19107
(215) 922-5483
www.thetroc.com

Trocadero
Directions: Located at 10th and Arch, right by the Friendship Gate

This small concert venue, which usually features rock and pop performers, will interest the teens and pre-teens in the family.

KC's Pastries Inc.

145 N. 11th St.
Philadelphia, PA 19107
(215) 351-1177

K C's Pastries Inc.
Directions: Across the street from the Pennsylvania Convention Center.

This shop has delicious pastries and other treats (try the raisin scones!) for less than a dollar each. Kids tend to like the bubble pearl drinks—smoothies and iced milk with little round (edible) pellets that seem to bounce around on the drink's surface.

Chinese Cultural Center

125 N. 10th St.
Philadelphia, PA
(215) 923-6767

Chinese Cultural Center
Directions: From Market Street, take 10th Street two blocks north.

From February to May, you can celebrate the Chinese New Year with a ten course banquet here.

Convention Center

Philadelphia Convention Center

1101 Arch St
Philadelphia, PA 19107
(800) 428-9000
www.paconvention.com

Lots of big events are held at the convention center, from the Philadelphia International Auto Show in January to the Mummers Fest in December. Most events are open to the public (at least partially), so be sure to watch the website for upcoming events. One of the biggest annual highlights is the Philadelphia Flower Show. Every March, hundreds of thousands of people travel from across the country to see the Flower Show, the world's largest horticultural event of its kind. Even when no events are scheduled, the Convention Center itself is still an interesting place, with its incredible collection of modern art. To my surprise, my kids actually enjoyed seeing the paintings, sculptures, jewelry and other artwork—they thought the "Cat with Scissors" and "Lizard Box" pieces were especially cool.

Reading Terminal Market

12th and Arch Streets
Philadelphia, PA 19107
(215) 922-2317
www.readingterminalmarket.org

Reading Terminal Market

Hours: Mon-Sat, 8 am-6 pm

Directions: From the Liberty Bell, take Market Street about eight blocks west.

The Market is home to almost 100 merchants (three of whom are descendants of original standholders from when the Market first opened in 1892). The Market itself is a historical wonder—it's basically the cellar of the Reading Railroad train shed. The Market is the third most popular Philly tourist attraction (after the Liberty Bell and Independence Hall) and I can certainly see why. You can truly find something to please everyone here. African crafts, Amish crafts and ethnic foods—you name it. It's best to go between Wed. and Sat., when Amish merchants are there.

Jim McWilliams/ Philadelphia
Convention & Visitors Bureau

Chapter Four

Parkway Museum District

The grandeur of the mansions in this section of Philadelphia often lulls tourists into a false sense of security. In truth, the north and west regions of the city contain some high-poverty areas and some basically rough neighborhoods. The area is pretty safe during the day, but changes rather radically after dark. There's a fairly high crime rate (compared to the Center City and Old City sections) and a considerable homeless population. In short, I wouldn't recommend wandering (or waiting for public transportation) in this area at night if you're not familiar with the neighborhood. That's generally not a problem, though, as most of the attractions close by early evening, so tourists tend to start heading back to their hotels before dark.

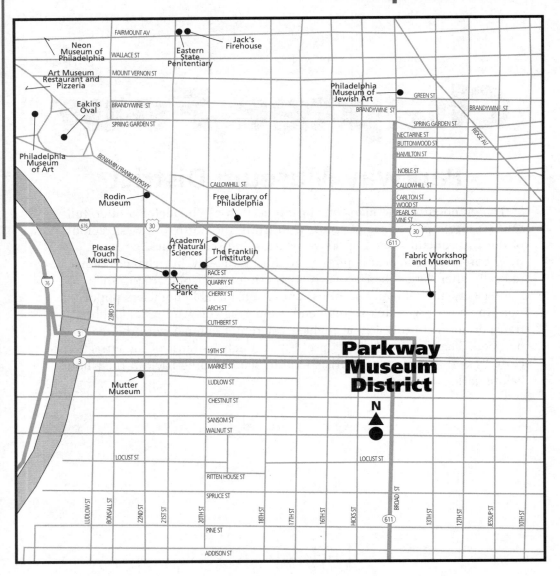

Neon Museum of Philadelphia

FAIRMOUNT AV

Jack's Firehouse

Eastern State Penitentiary

WALLACE ST

Art Museum Restaurant and Pizzeria

MOUNT VERNON ST

Philadelphia Museum of Jewish Art

GREEN ST

Eakins Oval

BRANDYWINE ST

BRANDYWINE ST

BRANDYWINE ST

SPRING GARDEN ST

SPRING GARDEN ST

RIDGE AV

NECTARINE ST

BUTTONWOOD ST

Philadelphia Museum of Art

BENJAMIN FRANKLIN PKWY

HAMILTON ST

NOBLE ST

CALLOWHILL ST

CALLOWHILL ST

Rodin Museum

Free Library of Philadelphia

CARLTON ST

WOOD ST

PEARL ST

VINE ST

676

30

611

30

Please Touch Museum

Academy of Natural Sciences

The Franklin Institute

Fabric Workshop and Museum

76

RACE ST

QUARRY ST

Science Park

CHERRY ST

ARCH ST

CUTHBERT ST

23RD ST

3

19TH ST

Parkway
Museum
District

3

MARKET ST

Mutter Museum

LUDLOW ST

CHESTNUT ST

N

SANSOM ST

WALNUT ST

LOCUST ST

LOCUST ST

RITTEN HOUSE ST

SPRUCE ST

LUDLOW ST

BONSALL ST

22ND ST

21ST ST

20TH ST

18TH ST

17TH ST

16TH ST

HICKS ST

BROAD ST

611

13TH ST

12TH ST

JESSUP ST

10TH ST

PINE ST

ADDISON ST

Parkway Museum District

Benjamin Franklin Parkway

The Benjamin Franklin Parkway was built to connect Fairmount Park with the center of the city. The boulevard stretches from City Hall to the Philadelphia Museum of Art and its design was inspired by the Avenue des Champs-Elysees in Paris. The Parkway is lined with flowerbeds, trees, fountains, hotels and restaurants. It is home to many of the city's large cultural institutions, including The Franklin Institute Science

The Mummer's Parade

Museum, the Please Touch Museum, the Rodin Museum, the Academy of Natural Sciences and the Free Library of Philadelphia. This is a popular spot for walking, running and skating, so pack your gear if you have room. Bike paths along Kelly Drive on the east side of the Schuylkill River and at West River Drive, on the west side, are prime spots for biking and outdoor jaunts. If you don't want to "schlep" your own stuff around, rent in-line skates at Boathouse Row on Kelly Drive behind the Philadelphia Museum of Art (the steps which *Rocky* made famous).

Note

This is often a congested area, especially during weekday rush hours, so be very careful when crossing the streets. Also, I've noticed that some of the pedestrian crossing signals aren't exactly generous with the time allotments, so don't dawdle when crossing the street.

We love to wander this area in the spring or summer, when the trees are in full bloom and the river is busy with activity. You can easily plan to spend most of the day in this neighborhood—even if you never step foot inside a single museum. The scenery (not to mention the beautiful mansions along Kelly Drive) are so lovely; I could easily just relax and people-watch the day away.

Fun Fact

Kelly Drive is named after Grace Kelly's father, John B. Kelly Sr., who served as president of the Fairmount Parks Commission years ago.

Logan Circle

Logan Circle

Directions: From JFK Plaza, take the Ben Franklin Parkway four blocks northwest.

Although it's now called Logan Circle, this is actually one of William Penn's "five squares" that he used in plotting out the city's design. Originally a morbid place (it was used for public hangings), it's now a beautiful section of the city. Logan Circle is home to some incredible pieces of outdoor art. Probably the most well-known are the three spouting bronze figures of the **Swann Memorial Fountain**, crafted and cast in 1924 by Alexander Stirling Calder, whose father created the statue of Penn atop City Hall. A lot of the benches close to the attractions face away from the fountain. I guess those would be good spots for watching the traffic and the passersby—but I prefer gazing at the fountain (it gives me that feeling of peace and tranquility that can be a precious commodity when traveling with several kids). Like all children, my kids love the fountain, and they really like the bronze frogs and turtles that shoot water from the basin.

Jim McWilliams/ Philadelphia Convention & Visitors Bureau

Logan Circle

Parkway Museum District

Museums

Academy of Natural Sciences

1900 Benjamin Franklin Parkway
Philadelphia, PA 19103
(215) 299-1000
www.acnatsci.org

Academy of Natural Sciences

Hours: Mon-Fri 10 am-4:30 pm;
Sat, Sun & Holidays 10 am-5 pm

Cost: Adults $9; Children $8;
Seniors $8.25

My kids' favorite part of this museum is Dinosaur Hall, where kids grow wide-eyed at the sight of dinosaur skeletons. They can also check out the "time machine" and take part in an archeological dig. I also like the butterfly exhibit and the tropical rain forest area.

Rich Dunoff/ Philadelphia Convention & Visitors Bureau

Academy of Natural Sciences

Chapter Four

Eastern State Penitentiary

2124 Fairmount Avenue
Philadelphia, PA 19130
(215) 236-3300
www.easternstate.org

Opened in 1829, Eastern State Penitentiary was part of a controversial movement to control inmates through a combination of confinement and labor. This massive prison—with its three-story-high walls—was considered the ultimate in correctional facilities back in its heyday. The ESP housed some of the country's most infamous criminals, including Al Capone and Willie Sutton. The penitentiary closed its doors in 1971 and was basically abandoned (although the caretaker reportedly continued to care for a family of stray cats that lived on the property). Finally in 1984, the Redevelopment Authority took control of the building, and thanks to funding from the Pew Charitable Trusts, began work to preserve the building. Still, it remains pretty much in its dark, deteriorating condition (you must wear hard hats for the tour) and may be too creepy for some kids. In fact, the ESP was the setting up for an episode of the MTV show, *Fear*, in which a team of six people would win $5,000 if they could remain in the dark penitentiary alone for thirty-six hours. Several of those people proclaimed the experience "terrifying." Maybe it's a good thing, then, that children under seven aren't allowed inside.

If you're not scared, the ESP is a fascinating place. There are hundreds of artifacts and supplies from the facility and its former prisoners. Two cells have been restored to tell the stories of a pair of prisoners who were housed at the ESP at different time periods. The ESP hosts Halloween ghost tours and Bastille Day events.

Eastern State Penitentiary
Hours: May, Sep, Oct, Sat-Sun 10 am-5 pm; Jun-Aug, Wed-Sun 10 am-5 pm
Ages: 7 and up
Cost: Adults $7; Students/Seniors $5; Children (7-17) $3
Directions: From the Art Museum, take 22nd Street five blocks north to Fairmount Avenue.

Hollywood Tidbit
The penitentiary "played the part" of the insane asylum in the movie *12 Monkeys*.

Parkway Museum District

The Franklin Institute

222 North 20th Street
Philadelphia, PA 19103
(215) 448-1200
www.sln.fi.edu/

The Franklin Institute
Hours: Daily 9:30 am-5 pm
Cost: Adults $12; Children $9. Imax, add $4

My kids really like the Sports Challenge section, where they can practice their skiing, golf, rock climbing and other athletic skills while learning about the physical process their bodies are experiencing during the activity. The spirit of the Institute's namesake (Ben Franklin) is very evident—

Rich Dunoff/Franklin Institute Science Museum

there are many exhibits and activities involving electricity. Once you see a film at the IMAX Theater, a trip to the normal movie theater will pale in comparison. The SkyBike looks very cool, although none of us have actually taken the plunge and tried it yet. You can also walk through a large model of the human heart. However, it's a pretty tight squeeze, so Jack has to wait outside with all the other big guys. And Brandon actually found the experience pretty scary. So, the members of your family who are a little "husky," claustrophobic or easily frightened may want to skip this experience.

Chapter Four

Mutter Museum

19 South 22nd Street
Philadelphia, PA 19103
(215) 563-3737 ext. 242
www.collphyphil.org/muttpg1.shtml

Mutter Museum
Hours: Daily, 10 am-5 pm
Ages: 6 and up
Cost: Adults $8; Children (6 and up) $5

While this museum's exhibits are definitely informative, they're also…well, pretty darn gross. The Mutter Museum is basically devoted to medical mutations and other physical oddities. There are hundreds of anatomical models made out of plaster, wax and various other materials. But there's also the real thing—hundreds of human skulls, and almost a thousand assorted body parts preserved in fluid-filled jars. My kids are pretty grossed out by the whole thing (although it was a lucky break when we happened to visit while the museum had a special exhibit on conjoined twins, just as John was working on a school research paper on the topic). But if your kids like horror movies or other gory stuff, this will be their idea of heaven.

Edward Savaria Jr./ Philadelphia Convention & Visitors Bureau

Parkway Museum District

Neon Museum of Philadelphia

860 N. 26th Street
Philadelphia, PA 19130
(215) 232-0478

Philadelphia neon designer, artist, preservationist, and collector Len Davidson has been fascinated with neon since his childhood. In 1985, he founded the Neon Museum of Philadelphia to showcase his collection of vintage neon; many of which he has restored to their original grandeur. Davidson has amassed some great pieces in his collection—such as a cool pink and green 1930s neon sign that used to adorn the Termini Bakery in South Philly. Although, the museum is currently looking for a permanent home and doesn't really have regular viewing hours for the public—Davidson is usually thrilled to show off his collection, if you ask nicely (and offering to buy a copy or two of his book on neon signs wouldn't hurt).

Philadelphia Museum of Art

26th Street and Ben Franklin Pkwy
Philadelphia, PA 19130
(215) 763-8100
www.philamuseum.org

Rich Dunoff/Philadelphia Convention & Visitors Bureau

Chapter Four

Philadelphia Museum of Art

Hours: Tues-Sun 10 am-5 pm;
Wed-Thurs evenings
until 8:45 pm

Cost: Adults $10; Children
(13-18) $7, (12 and under) Free

Directions: Take Ben Franklin
Parkway all the way north,
and it'll lead directly to
the Art Museum.

Okay, okay, let's get this out of the way—you know you want to do it, so go ahead! I'm talking, of course, about the "Rocky run." Stand at the bottom of the huge set of steps, take a deep breath and go for it. Don't worry, onlookers will barely bat an eyelash. Locals are so used to wacky people running (or attempting to run) up the steps and acting like crazy lunatics that it doesn't even faze them. And as for other tourists—well, they're just timidly waiting for someone else to go first, so they can work up the nerve to do it, too. Nick, Brandon and John have all done it (although they may have taken a few breaks on the way up) complete with the grand finale of dancing around at the top with your fists in the air.

To the dismay of many artists and art lovers, the museum is destined to remain forever overshadowed by the "Italian Stallion," because to some people, what's inside the building will never be as interesting as a set of stone steps. That's a shame, because the museum has some really exciting collections and exhibits. Those of you who venture past the steps and into the building will find many exciting things; such as textiles from Egypt, China, Turkey, Greece and the rest of the world. Our favorites include the armor collection and the Japanese teahouse.

The museum offers some great family programs on Sundays, many of which are free. Some recent and upcoming programs include Drawing Together, Explorer's Tour, Medieval Craft Demonstrations and Tales and Treasures.

Fun Facts
- For the record, there are ninety-nine steps at the museum's front entrance.
- Although Rocky's "footprints" still appear at the top of the museum steps, his statue was moved and now stands atop the steps at the First Union Spectrum.

Parkway Museum District

Please Touch Museum

210 North 21st Street
Philadelphia, PA 19103
(215) 963-0667
www.pleasetouchmuseum.com

This is definitely a "must see" Philly attraction for parents of young children. (Hint: if you'll be in Philly for several days, plan your Old City tour for the sunniest day, and keep the kids busy inside at the Please Touch Museum on the rainy day.) The museum tends to be busiest in the morning, when school groups are most likely to visit. You will have to park your stroller at the lobby entrance, but the museum will lend you a Snuglie to carry your baby. If you don't want to eat in the museum's lounge (where basically you're limited to vending machine food), you can get your hand stamped, grab a bite at one of the nearby restaurants, and then come back to the museum. The museum also hosts kids' birthday parties.

There are lots of cool things here for kids to do, and—as the name implies—many of them involve "hands on" activities. I like the fact that the exhibits and activities are both fun and educational. The Alice in Wonderland area, for example, helps kids practice their reading and language skills. My kids always liked the mini TV studio that lets them pretend to be stars. Kids also really love the pretend supermarket where kids can scan their "groceries." While the Please Touch Museum is sure to be a hit with younger kids, children over age eight or so may become bored fairly quickly. My only complaint is that you have to pay full admission price for adults and older kids, who will basically be doing a lot of standing around and watching the little ones have all the fun.

> **Please Touch Museum**
>
> Hours: Daily 9 am-4:30 pm
> Jul 1-Labor Day, Daily 9 am-5:30 pm
>
> Cost: $8.95; Age one and under free
>
> Directions: Take Benjamin Franklin Parkway to 21st Street, then go two blocks on 21st Street.

Chapter Four

Science Park

21st and Race Streets
Philadelphia, PA 19103
(215) 963-0667

Science Park was created via a partnership between the Please Touch Museum and the Franklin Institute. It's a great outdoor science-oriented learning area, where kids can check out such exhibits as "Whispering Tubes" and "Energy Golf."

Science Park

Hours: Open Memorial Day to Labor Day, with hours coinciding with the Please Touch Museum

Directions: Located across the street from the Please Touch Museum.

Cost: Free with Admission to Please Touch Museum

Rodin Museum

Benjamin Franklin Parkway at 22nd Street
Philadelphia, PA 19101
(215) 763-8100
www.rodinmuseum.org

This museum houses a huge collection of works by the famous French sculptor Auguste Rodin. It's very impressive, but probably not the most exciting experience from a kid's point of view. However, they all seem to get a kick out of the statue of The Thinker in front of the museum.

Rodin Museum

Hours: Tues-Sun 10 am-5 pm

Cost: $3 (suggested donation)

Directions: Take Benjamin Franklin Parkway north to 22nd Street.

Fabric Workshop and Museum

1315 Cherry Street
Philadelphia, PA 19107
(215) 568-1111
www.fabricworkshop.org

This very small, unique museum has rotating exhibits that focus on fabric design, use, and artistic qualities. It's a bright, open space with tall divider walls that hold the display cases.

Fabric Workshop and Museum

Hours: Mon-Fri 9 am-6 pm; Sun 12 pm-4 pm

Ages: 3 and up

Cost: Free

Parkway Museum District

Philadelphia Museum of Jewish Art

615 N. Broad St.
Philadelphia, PA 19123
(215) 627-6747

Features paintings, wooden figures and other artistic creations with a Jewish theme. I wasn't even familiar with Jewish art before visiting this museum, so it definitely enlightened me.

> **Philadelphia Museum of Jewish Art**
>
> Hours: Mon-Thurs 10 am-3 pm;
> Fri 10 am-1 pm
>
> Cost: free

Where to Eat

The emphasis in this part of town is definitely on art and architecture, not dining and shopping. Frankly, good places to eat and shop are in short supply here, at least in comparison to the rest of the city. But you'll work up an appetite touring all these museums and mansions, so here are a few suggestions as to where you can stop and refuel your hungry brood.

Jack's Firehouse

2130 Fairmount Ave
Philadelphia, PA 19130
(215) 232-9000

> **Jack's Firehouse**
>
> Directions: Take Fairmount Avenue west to 21st Street.

Located inside a real Victorian firehouse (complete with brass pole), Jack's is definitely an unforgettable dining experience. Aside from the building itself, there's the menu—which features such unusual fare as bison, beaver tail and buffalo with moonshine sauce. Don't worry, there's also the tamer stuff like sandwiches and macaroni with tomato sauce.

Art Museum Restaurant and Pizzeria

24th and Fairmount Ave.
Philadelphia, PA 19130
(215) 765-7250

Located around the corner from the Art Museum, this small corner eatery offers some good Italian dishes (try the stromboli!).

Chapter Four

Other Places of Interest

Smith Civil War Memorial

N. Concourse Drive
Philadelphia, PA 19130
(215) 685-0000

> **Smith Civil War Memorial**
>
> Directions: In Fairmount Park, take N. Concourse Drive south towards the river. The Civil War Memorial is just past Memorial Hall.

Foundry owner Richard Smith built this memorial between 1897 and 1912 to honor Pennsylvania's Civil War heroes, including Generals Hancock, Meade and Reynolds. Locals are fond of the "Whispering Benches," located at the base of the Memorial Arch. The Whispering Benches are designed in such a way that if a person sitting at one end of the long bench turns and whispers into the wall behind him, another person all the way at the other end of the bench can hear what was said. During the day, this is a popular spot with families enjoying picnics (and kids testing out the benches). Local legend has it that this is a lucky spot to get your first kiss, so at night it tends to be filled with teenagers and others in the throes of romance.

Eakins Oval

Located at the end of Ben Franklin Parkway, next to the Philadelphia Art Museum.

Contrary to what some locals believe, Eakins Oval doesn't exist simply to make driving in the area more challenging. The paved center serves as a backup parking area for the museum, and is also a concert venue and seating area for festivals and major events. At the end of the oval by the museum are several fountains featuring George Washington on a horse, various animals, and more.

Free Library of Philadelphia

19th and Vine
Logan Square
Philadelphia, PA 19107
(215) 686-5322

In addition to offering lots of books for loan, the Free Library has some amazing literary collections. The Rare Books Department is a really interesting museum (it's also the final resting place of Charles Dickens's pet raven, Grip). The library offers lots of great activities and programs. Sundays on Stage, for example, is an afternoon program geared specifically toward families.

Chapter Five

Down South

Philly's southern region basically boils down to two all-important topics: sports and food—with a little funky South Street flavor thrown in for good measure.

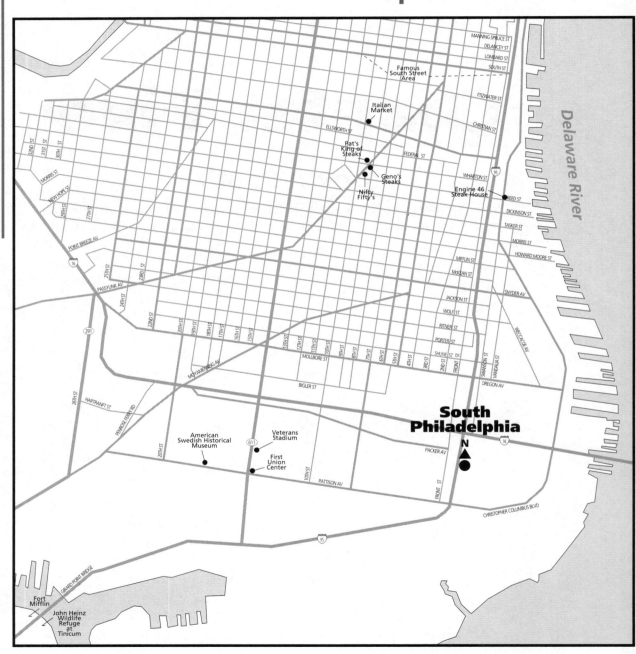

Down South

South Street

Between Front & 11th on South Street
www.south-street.com

This area will probably be of more interest to families with teens and preteens because of its "hip factor" (as in, you'll see hairdos in a wild array of different styles and colors, usually sported by people with numerous tattoos and perhaps a few body-piercings). However, even younger kids often get a kick out of people-watching and checking out all the colorful characters (there are often jugglers, singers, and other street performers wandering around in warmer weather). To

avoid any embarrassing incidents, you might want to have a little talk with your kids first, warning them that they'll see a lot of "unique" people. This will make them less likely to point or stare.

Although this area can get pretty crowded (picture a lot of teens just "hanging out"), I like its eclectic Greenwich Village–type of "vibe." And, hey, if you suddenly get the urge to get your bellybutton pierced while on a family vacation, this is your lucky day (just kidding!).

Edward Savaria Jr/ Philadelphia Convention & Visitors Bureau

The Italian Market

South Ninth Street between Christian and Wharton Streets
Philadelphia, PA 19147
(215) 334-6008

The Italian Market

Hours: Tues-Sun 9 am-4 pm

Edward Savaria Jr/ Philadelphia Convention & Visitors Bureau

Founded by Italian immigrants in the early 1900s, this market is truly an experience that you can't miss. You can buy great fresh produce, of course, but there are also specialty foods, gourmet items, cheese, spices, meats—not to mention the ample advice and recipes from the helpful vendors. With all the laughing, activity, and lots of Italian conversation, this reminds me of a scene from an old movie (and, in fact, the Italian Market was featured heavily in the movie *Rocky*). One word of caution: live animals such as chickens and crabs are in plain sight, waiting to be "selected." The thought of these animals becoming someone's dinner was very upsetting to my kids. If your kids are on the sensitive side, you might want to try to steer them away from anyone who may be getting ready to make their selection from among a still-breathing inventory.

Down South

Sports and Entertainment

People in Philly take their sports seriously. Fortunately, by taking a quick trip to the south side of town, you can satisfy any sports-related desire you could possibly have. Football? No problem. Baseball? We gotcha covered. Hockey? Basketball? Soccer? Yep, sure thing.

Philly also hosts a ton of sports-related events each year. For example, in April, there are the NCAA men's gymnastics championships. In June, it's the senior PGA championships and the NBA "Hoop It Up" tournament. Also, get your running shoes on in November, because that's Philadelphia marathon time.

First Union Center (and First Union Spectrum)

3601 S. Broad Street
Philadelphia, PA 19148
(215) 336-3600
www.comcast-spectacor.com

Len Redkoles/ Philadelphia Convention & Visitors Bureau

Home of the **Flyers**, the **Kixx**, and the **76ers**, First Union offers self-guided tours of the Flyers history from 1967 through the present day, with authentic artifacts, memorabilia and images. Interactive kiosks, presented by Comcast, guide you through some of the greatest moments in Flyers history, player profiles, and upcoming events. Basketball fans can visit the 76ers Zone, read quotes from the Greats, see highlights, player profiles, and view the community calendar. Want the full royal treatment? Choose a guided tour, and you'll explore the private

Chapter Five

luxury seating levels, the press box, Arena Vision studio control room, Comcast SportsNet, and the official NBA and NHL locker rooms.

In addition to sporting events, First Union also hosts shows such as "Disney on Ice", as well as concerts (I'm looking forward to seeing Bon Jovi here this spring).

Even though I'll give you information about the venues, I won't go into too much detail here about the specific teams because (a) most readers will probably know much more about the teams than I do, and (b) I'm including information about each team's website, which offers the most current information.

First Union Center
Box Office hours: Mon-Fri 9 am-6 pm; Sat 10 am-4:30 pm; Sun (event day only) 10 am-4:30 pm
Ages: 4 and up
Tours: Adults $6; Children $5
Directions: Take I-76 East and follow the signs for South Jersey, Walt Whitman Bridge and Sports Complex. Continue East to exit 45, Broad Street, Sports Complex. At the bottom of the exit ramp, make a right onto Broad Street. The First Union Center will be on your left.

Philadelphia 76ers

3601 S. Broad Street
Philadelphia, PA 19148
(215) 952-7000
www.nba.com/sixers

Philadelphia 76ers
Season runs Oct-Apr
Cost: $12-$53

Philadelphia's NBA team. The season runs from October through April. Season tickets are available in a variety of plans, including full-season ($516-$1,290), half-season ($294-$714), twelve game ($180-$444), and ten game ($150-$370).

Philadelphia Flyers

3601 S. Broad Street
Philadelphia, PA 19148
(215)465-4500
www.philadelphiaflyers.com

Philadelphia Flyers
Season runs Oct-Apr
Ages: 5 and up
Cost: $23-$80

Philadelphia's NHL team.

Philadelphia Kixx

3601 S. Broad Street
Philadelphia, PA 19148
(888) 888KIXX
www.kixxonline.com

Philadelphia Kixx
Ages: 4 and up
Cost: $16-$18

Philadelphia's soccer team.

Down South

Philadelphia Phantoms

3601 S. Broad Street
Philadelphia, PA 19148
(215) 465-4522
www.phantomshockey.com

The Philadelphia's hockey team. A **family value pack** ticket deal is available: four tickets, four hot dogs, and four sodas for $48.

Bowie Baysox

3601 S. Broad Street
Philadelphia, PA 19148
(301) 805-2233
www.baysox.com

The Bowie Baysox Baseball Club is the Class AA affiliate of the Baltimore Orioles.

Wings Lacrosse Team

First Union
www.comcast-spectacor.com/sports/wingssche.asp

Veterans Stadium

3501 South Broad Street
Philadelphia, PA 19148
(215) 463-6000

Until the new park is built, is home base for the Phillies baseball team and the Eagles football team.

Philadelphia Phillies

3501 South Broad Street
Philadelphia, PA 19148
(215) 463-1000
www.phillies.mlb.com

The Phillies, Philadelphia's baseball team, play at Veteran's Stadium...for now. A new field is being built and is set to open in spring of 2004. New ballpark will be constructed just east of Veterans Stadium, on the north side of Pattison Avenue between 11th and Darien Streets in South Philadelphia, and will span a twenty-one acre site.

Chapter Five

Philadelphia Eagles

3501 South Broad Street
Philadelphia, PA 19148
(215) 463-5500
www.philadelphiaeagles.com

Philadelphia Eagles

Season runs Sept-Jan

Philadelphia's National Football League team plays, for now, at Veterans Stadium, but is scheduled to be at Lincoln Field by August 2003.

Lincoln Financial Field

Scheduled to open in August 2003, this will be the new home of the Philadelphia Eagles. The Lincoln Financial Field will have state-of-the-art features including improved seating and sight lines, dramatic entertainment systems, an exterior plaza, club and luxury seating.

Philadelphia Phillies Ballpark

With a target opening date of April 2004, the new ballpark is being touted as a "complete sports entertainment experience." New ballpark will be constructed just east of Veterans Stadium, on the north side of Pattison Avenue between 11th and Darien Streets in South Philadelphia, and will span a twenty-one acre site.

Down South

Museums

American Swedish Historical Museum

1900 Pattison Avenue
Philadelphia, PA 19145
(215) 389-1776
www.americanswedish.org

This unique museum, located in FDR Park near Veterans Stadium, hosts permanent and temporary exhibits celebrating twentieth century Swedish interior design. Several rooms in this large mansion depict various eras and help visitors to get a feel for both the people and style of that period.

> **American Swedish Historical Museum**
>
> Hours: Tues-Fri 10 am-4 pm;
> Sat-Sun 12 pm-4 pm
>
> Cost: Adults $5;
> Children (12-18) $4

Mummers Museum

1100 South 2nd Street
Philadelphia, PA 19147
(215) 336-3050
www.riverfrontmummers.com/museum.html

The Mummers Museum opened in 1976 and is dedicated to the Philadelphia celebration of New Years. The museum houses a rich collection of Mummers' paraphernalia and memorabilia. Basically, you'll see more feathers, sequins, and loud colors than you've ever imagined. Every Tuesday evening, from May through September, the Museum holds a free outdoor String Band Concert. It's like an old-fashioned block party; you can bring a lawn chair, munch on Philly soft pretzels and hot dogs, and sip on some soda. Then sit back and listen to a famous String Band, join the dancers, and learn the "Mummers Strut."

> **Mummers Museum**
>
> Hours: Oct-Apr Tues-Sat 9:30 am-5 pm;
> Sun 12 pm-5 pm; May-Sept,
> Tue 9:30 am-9:30 pm;
> Wed-Sat 9:30 am-5 pm;
> Sun 12 pm-5 pm
>
> Ages 5 and up
>
> Cost: Adults $2.50;
> Children (under 12) $2

Other Points of Interest

Fort Mifflin

Fort Mifflin Road
Philadelphia, PA 19153
(215) 685-4192
www.fortmifflin.org

Fort Mifflin is the only Fort in Philadelphia. It offers daily tours, great views, and a glimpse at history. In 1777, the Fort and its soldiers held back the British Navy for seven weeks in a decisive battle. Guides, in period costumes, provide stories and artifacts that help bring to life those harrowing weeks. Be warned: an artillery and weapons demonstration is held daily at 12:30 p.m. during the season (April through November), so be sure to hold your ears! A large moat surrounding the Fort features frogs and small fish which fascinates children of all ages.

> **Fort Mifflin**
>
> Hours: Apr 1-Nov 30, Wed-Sun 10 am-4 pm
>
> Adults $6; Children $3; Children (Under 3) Free
>
> Directions: I-95 North to exit 13, (West 291). Turn left on to Island Avenue. Then turn left on to Enterprise Avenue. Turn right on to Fort Mifflin Road. Proceed a mile to the first left. After the tunnel is the entrance to Fort Mifflin.

John Heinz Wildlife Refuge at Tinicum

86th St. & Lindbergh Blvd.
Philadelphia, PA 19153
(215) 365-3118
www.heinz.fws.gov

Largest tidal wetland in PA. Trails open all year for walking and good bird watching; over 280 species of birds have been spotted here.

> **John Heinz Wildlife Refuge at Tinicum**
>
> Hours: Outdoors—daily 8 am-sunset
> Visitor's Center—May-Sept., 9 am-4:30 pm, Oct-Apr, 8:30 am-4 pm
>
> Cost: Free

Philadelphia International Airport Tours

Terminal B at the airport
(215) 937-6747

Get a one-hour tour of the operation of the entire airport. A tour of the airfield by bus is also available.

> **Philadelphia International Airport Tours**
>
> Hours: Mon-Sat, 10 am-noon
>
> Cost: Free

Down South

Where to Eat

Engine 46 Steak House

10 Reed Street
Philadelphia, PA 19147
(215) 462-4646
www.engine46.com

Engine 46 Steak House

Hours: Sun-Thurs 11 am-12 pm;
Fri.-Sat 11 am-2 am

Directions: I-95 Exit 20 at
Columbus Blvd. and Reed Street.

   The food's good, but kids usually are so busy noticing the décor—a firehouse theme that includes fire hydrants, Dalmatian tablecloths, and even a pole—that they really don't notice their food. The menu features classic staples like steak, ribs, fresh seafood, chicken, and the kids' menu begins at $2.50.

Johnny Rockets

443 South Street
Philadelphia, PA 19147
(215) 829-9222

Johnny Rockets

Hours: Sun-Wed 11 am-11 pm;
Thurs 11 am-12 pm;
Fri-Sat 11 am-2 am

Directions: Take South Street
to the intersection with
E. Passyunk Avenue.

   Like something out of a scene from Happy Days, Johnny Rockets has the perfect 1950s type atmosphere with chrome counters and stools, oldies music, all-white uniforms for wait staff, and mostly traditional 50's America drive-in food. This is a nostalgic stop for burgers, chili, grilled chicken sandwiches, tuna salad, and great fries. The kids' menu includes hamburgers, hot dogs, chicken fingers, peanut butter and jelly, and grilled cheese. Don't miss the great old-fashioned malts, milkshakes, and homemade apple pie. High chairs and booster seats are available.

Nifty Fifty's

1356 Passyunk Ave.
Philadelphia, PA 19147
(215) 468-1950

Nifty Fifty's

Hours: Sun-Thurs, 6 am-11 pm;
Fri-Sat 6 am-1 am

Directions: Take 10th Street
south to Reed, and go to the
intersection with Passyunk.

   Another eatery with the 1950s feel, this diner comes complete with loud music and glaring neon lights—kids will appreciate the constant action. The food is good, and the house specialty is milkshakes. The wait can get long during prime hours (weekend mornings), but there are lots of penny candy machines to entertain the kids. High chairs and booster seats are available. There are no diaper-changing facilities in the restrooms.

Pat's King of Steaks

1237 Passayunk Avenue
Philadelphia, PA 19147
(215) 468-1546
www.patskingofsteaks.com

Pat's King of Steaks

Hours: Daily, 24 hours

Directions: Located on
Passyunk between 9th and
Wharton Streets

Between Pat's and Geno's across the street, this corner is paradise for cheesesteak lovers (and, no, I'm not crazy enough to take sides in the Pat's vs. Geno's debate). This world-renowned, family-owned restaurant offers the option of dining in or taking out cheesesteaks (in various versions), fries, fish sandwiches, and hot dogs. Open twenty-four hours a day, the place brims with people at all hours of the day and night. Grab a seat at the benches outside, if you can, and watch the world go by as you gulp down a sandwich.

Geno's Steaks

1219 S. Ninth St.
Philadelphia, PA 19147
(215) 389-0659
www.genosteaks.com

Geno's Steaks

Directions: Across the street from Pat's.
Take Ninth Street south to Passyunk.

You might as well call this "Cheesesteak Corner." Something to keep in mind at both Geno's and Pat's—it's basically like committing a mortal sin to request anything healthy (such as lettuce) on a cheesesteak. Don't ask how many calories are in anything, and don't even think about shooting a sideways glance at the roll while mentioning that you're watching your carbs.

If you don't believe me, try it for yourself, but of course I'll pretend not to know you as you're being "escorted" out the door. Really, though, if you wanted to eat something healthy, you wouldn't be chowing down on red meat that's been fried in onions and smothered with cheese—now, would you? Geno's offers thick beef slices with the usual toppings available (onions, peppers, provolone, Cheese Whiz).

Know Your Cheesesteak Code of Conduct!

Like their neighbor and cheesesteak rival—across the street, the guys at Geno's are pretty strict about this whole cheesesteak ordering process. Remember the Soup Nazi on Seinfeld? Well, substitute cheesesteaks for soup, throw in a whole lot of Philly attitude, and you've got the picture.

Basically, when it comes to ordering a cheesesteak, the main thing to remember is to keep it short and sweet. You're not at the Four Seasons ruminating with the wine steward over the best bottle of vintage bubbly. The guys at Pat's and Geno's don't want chit-chat (after all, they're busy waging a brutal neighborhood cheesesteak war). The guy taking your order just needs to know two things—your cheese preference, and whether or not you want onions. Convey that information in as few words as possible, and maybe your mug shot will be added to the "wall of fame" that each place maintains, featuring photos of famous (and infamous) people eating a cheesesteak from that establishment.

Chapter Six

To the West

Frankly, the western part of the city is kind of a mixed bag. It contains some of the roughest neighborhoods in town, and has relatively few tourist attractions compared to other parts of the city. On the other hand, certain western neighborhoods like Manayunk have recently been making efforts to revamp their image and become contenders for tourists' attention (and dollars).

I would advise touring the other parts of the city first to make sure you hit all the hot tourist spots, and then trekking to the west if you have time left. Then again, if you're not into the usual tourist scene, or if your kids are older teens that want to get a real taste of the big city, perhaps you'll want to check out some of these places first. Keep in mind that there are some high-crime areas in the western part of the city, so be alert and try to avoid the area at night. The one exception is "Third Thursdays." On the third Thursday of every month, businesses and attractions in West Philadelphia hold special programs from 5:00 p.m. to 8:30 p.m., with an emphasis on music, food and drink. The area is pretty safe during that period, although I'd still be careful to stick with the main tourist route and not stray too far from your intended destination.

Philadelphia Zoo

3400 West Girard Avenue
Philadelphia, PA 19104
(215) 243-1100
www.phillyzoo.org

Philadelphia Zoo

Hours: Feb-Nov Daily 9:30 am-5 pm; Dec-Jan; Daily 11 am-4 pm

Ages: 1 and up

Cost: Adults $10.95; Children $7.95

Directions: From Center City, take West River Drive to Sweet Briar Drive and turn left. At South Concourse Drive turn left and go one block to Girard Avenue.

The nations very first zoo was this one, dating back to the 1800s. On our first trip here, we were shocked when a peacock strutted right up to Brandon! Yes, they wander around freely (so keep alert!). The lines to get into the zoo can be very long, but if you have a CityPass (www.citypass.com) you can enter through a special gate. We usually save ourselves at least an hour in waiting time this way. Also, the easiest way to get here is by taking the PHLASH—it stops right at the front entrance every ten minutes throughout the day.

Brian Porco

My kids love monkeys, so they were thrilled to see the Primate Reserve. All sorts of monkeys, gorillas and other primates hang out here, climbing on ropes, up ladders, swinging from place to place and just putting on a show for visitors.

The zoo offers special behind-the-scenes "backstage tours" during the winter, so be sure to check their website for a schedule of upcoming events.

My only complaint about the zoo is the horribly long lines—both at the entrance and at the food counters. Considering how crowded the zoo can get (especially on weekends) I think the food facilities are woefully inadequate. My advice is to eat a big breakfast, and only plan on getting a quick snack at the zoo.

The latest addition is the amazing **Zoo Balloon**, which offers a birds-eye fifteen minute tour of the zoo and neighboring Fairmount Park. Order tickets in advance; weather permitting, the balloon operates Sun.-Wed. 9:30 a.m. to 5:00 p.m. and Thurs.-Sat. until 8:00 p.m. Tickets for those not visiting the zoo are $15.95 for adults and $12.95 for kids ages two to eleven. The balloon holds up to thirty people, and can even accommodate people in wheelchairs.

Tip
Come before 2:00 p.m. to be sure to see the widest variety of animals and to experience animal rides, boat rides and walk-through exhibits. Watch lion and tiger feedings weekdays at 3:00 p.m. and weekends at 4:00 p.m. (in season).

To the West

University City

Philadelphia is a big college town. In fact, Philly has about fifty colleges and universities—the second largest number of all cities in the U.S. However, unless your kids are old enough to be contemplating their college choices, that probably won't matter much to you as someone who is visiting the city. In fact, some tourist families see it as a drawback. Of course, with colleges come young people, who sometimes have a tendency to get a little rowdy. College campuses generally are not the most convenient places to try and push a stroller while lugging a diaper bag and trying to keep an eye on a few kids. Still, many of the campuses have some beautiful grounds (including expansive lawns that make great places for Frisbee or other game) and there are some interesting attractions that you might want to visit.

University Museum of Archaeology and Anthropology

33rd and Spruce Streets
Philadelphia, PA 19104
(215) 898-4000

If your kids liked the movie *The Mummy*, they'll love this place—it has mummies galore! You can check out tombs of Egyptian royalty, and see lots of ancient artifacts, icons, relics—and of course, the mummies. A new exhibit, *Worlds Intertwined: Etruscans, Greeks, and Romans*, opens in March 2003.

University Museum of Archaeology and Anthropology

Hours: Tues-Sat 10 am-4:30 pm; Sun 1 pm-5 pm

Cost: $5 adults, $2.50 seniors and non-Penn students; free for kids under 6 and Penn students

Directions: Located on the University of Pennsylvania campus. Take I-76 (Schuylkill Expressway) to the South Street exit (left lane exit). Turn west (right from the west; left from the east) at the light at the top of the exit ramp. The Museum is on the left past the next light.

Tip

Admission is free on Sunday, but the museum is closed Sundays from Memorial Day through Labor Day.

The Fairmount Park Area

Fairmount Park

Follow Ben Franklin Parkway all the way north, and you'll reach something that might surprise you, considering it's smack dab in the middle of a major city. Fairmount Park, the world's largest landscaped city park, consists of almost 9,000 acres of greenery, lakes, bike paths and lots more. The Schuylkill River divides Fairmount Park into east and west sections.

This is the perfect place for countless family activities—Frisbee games, picnics, bike rides, tennis, swimming, fishing or whatever else strikes your fancy. The Park Commission hosts all kinds of great activities—weekly bike rides in conjunction with the Bicycle Club, summer day camps for kids, Ultimate Frisbee every night in the summer, folk dancing, juggling, rowing and more.

Jim McWilliams/Philadelphia Convention & Visitors Bureau

Fun Fact
"Faire Mount" is actually the hill on which the Art Museum now stands.

To the West

Jim McWilliams/Philadelphia Convention & Visitors Bureau

Kelly Drive

Kelly Drive winds around the east side of the river in the Fairmount Park area. This is the route you'll take to access most of the mansions on the east side of the park. Along the way, you'll pass some cherry blossom trees and other colorful scenery, as well as a succession of statues and art pieces. My favorites are the Joan of Arc statue and the Playing Angels (a trio of angel statues, which my kids always jokingly say represent them, because they're such—ahem—angels).

Fun Fact
Kelly Drive is named after Grace Kelly's father, John B. Kelly Sr., who served as president of the Fairmount Parks Commission many years ago.

The Water Works

Kelly Drive, Fairmount Park
(215) 581-5111

The Water Works

Directions: Go around
the Art Museum and
continue on Kelly Drive
to the Water Works.

Philadelphia's National Historic Landmark. For most of the nineteenth century, the Water Works (with the help of steam engines, water wheels and water turbines) supplied the city of Philadelphia with a constant water supply. I couldn't tell you exactly what function the Water Works serves today (okay, I probably could if I tried), but to me it just needs to sit there and look cool. It also reminds me of a scene from the Hollywood movie, Spartacus or some other Greek/Roman epic.

Edward Savaria Jr/Philadelphia Convention & Visitors Bureau

To the West

Boathouse Row

Kelly Drive, East Fairmount Park
Philadelphia, PA 19130
(215) 769-9693

Boathouse Row

Directions: Take Kelly
Drive past the Water
Works.

    Easily one of the most beautiful riverside scenes I've ever seen, Boathouse Row seemed created specifically to become a classic Philadelphia postcard. The row of boathouses (originally built for the city's rowing clubs) line the east bank of the Schuylkill River, and are outlined at night by a string of white lights. The best view we've found is from atop the Art Museum steps.

    The fifteen houses that now line Boathouse Row (including one or two dating back to around 1860) feature a variety of architectural styles. Gothic Revival and Italianate styles first marked the site. Most of the houses built in the 1870s and early 1880s exhibited an ornamental Victorian Gothic style associated with the Philadelphia Centennial buildings elsewhere in Fairmount Park. No new boathouse has been built since 1904.

Edward Savaria Jr/Philadelphia Convention & Visitors Bureau

The Mansions

Fairmount Park is also home to more than two dozen incredible Colonial mansions, all of which are open to the public (individual schedules vary). The mansions are all under the jurisdiction of the Fairmount Park Commission, although other groups or businesses maintain many of them. For example, the Philadelphia Museum of Art maintains Strawberry Mansion, Laurel Hill, Lemon Hill, Cedar Grove, Mount Pleasant, Woodford and Sweetbriar. If your kids are very young or have really short attention spans, you may want to limit your mansion tours to a few at a time—to keep the kids from getting too restless. Here are some of the mansions you may want to visit:

Belmont Mansion

Belmont Mansion Drive
Philadelphia, PA 19131
(215) 878-8844

Belmont Mansion

Hours: Tours by appointment

Directions: From Kelly Drive, take Strawberry Mansion Bridge across the river, stay to the left on Chamounix Drive. Take two more left turns, and you'll be on Belmont Mansion Drive.

Belmont Mansion was the eighteenth and nineteenth century home of the Peters family. William Peters, and upper-class English lawyer who handled property management matters for the Penn family, bought the property in 1742. Belmont mansion has that Georgian look often found in homes of upper-class Americans of the Colonial period. Like other examples of its class, Belmont sits proudly at the crest of its hill overlooking the Schuylkill River. Some highlights of the mansion's interior include the paneled and carved woodwork and the elaborate molded plaster ceilings. Be sure to check out the woodwork and plaster in the hall.

To the West

Mount Pleasant

Mt. Pleasant Drive
Philadelphia, PA 19131
(215) 235-7469

Mount Pleasant actually consists of three buildings—the main house in the middle, and then identical smaller "plantation" houses on both sides. Built in the 1760s by a successful Scottish sea captain named John Macpherson, the home features some of the most impressive carved woodwork you'll ever see. The home is maintained by the Philadelphia Museum of Art, which has furnished the home with authentic period pieces, including some from the museum's Chippendale collection.

Mount Pleasant
Fee: $3
Hours: Tues-Sun 10 am-5 pm
Directions: Take Kelly Drive past the Angels Statue.

Fun Fact

The list of people who have owned this property reads like a "Who's Who" of Philadelphia high society. Benedict Arnold bought Mount Pleasant as a wedding gift for his bride, but he was convicted of treason before they could occupy it. Another owner was a great-nephew of Ben Franklin.

Cedar Grove

Lansdowne Drive
Philadelphia, PA 19131
(215) 763-8100

This was a Quaker farmhouse originally built in 1748. In 1926, Lydia Thompson Morris, fifth generation owner of Cedar Grove, had the house dismantled stone by stone and rebuilt in Fairmount Park as her gift to the city. The furnishings are a wonderful assortment of pieces collected over three centuries by five generations.

Cedar Grove
Fee: $3
Hours: Tues-Sun 10 am-5 pm
Directions: Turn left at the Smith Civil War Memorial.

I like the two-sided wall of closets upstairs. It might not be apparent to those of us who are spoiled by modern day conveniences, but the kitchen actually contains several items that were considered innovative during the 1700s, such as an indoor oven and a hot water boiler.

Chapter Six

Chamounix

Chamounix Drive
Philadelphia, PA 19131
(215) 878-3676

A two-and-a-half story brick and stone Federal style house, Chamounix was built in the early-1800s by George Plumstead, a wealthy Philadelphia Quaker merchant. The home currently serves as a youth hostel (you can rent a room for under $20 a night, but you have to share a bathroom with other guests). It has some great antique furnishings, and you can also spot some old sketches and maps.

> **Chamounix**
>
> Directions: From Kelly Drive, take the Strawberry Mansion Bridge across the river and stay to your left on Chamounix Drive.

Japanese Tea House
(also known as Shofuso or Pine Breeze Villa)

West Fairmount Park
Philadelphia, PA 19131
(215) 878-5097

This authentic and exquisite reconstruction of a seventeenth century Japanese scholar's house, tea house and garden was actually placed in this spot in 1958. It was designed according to traditional standards and built in Japan in 1953, and was then exhibited at the Museum for Modern Art in New York City for two years. The house was then given to the Fairmount Park Commission to replace the Japanese temple gate that had occupied this spot for many years. Be sure to check out the roof—it's made from the bark of hinoki, which grows only in Japan. For a really memorable experience, try to time your visit to coincide with a traditional tea ceremony.

> **Japanese Tea House (also known as Shofuso or Pine Breeze Villa)**
>
> Fee: $2.50
>
> Hours: Open May-Oct, Tues-Sun 10 am-4 pm
>
> Directions: From Belmont mansion Drive, go around the Horticulture Center.

To the West

Sweetbriar

Lansdowne Drive
Philadelphia, PA 19131
(215) 222-1333

Built in 1797, this three-story Federal style mansion remains in its original form, complete with many furnishings that belonged to its original owner, Samuel Breck. You feel like an aristocrat as you walk down the entry hallway and then catch sight of the stairway with its balcony and inset arched niche. I love all the elegant touches, like the candelabra and the French clock.

Fun Fact

Samuel Breck and his wife originally built Sweetbriar in an attempt to escape Yellow Fever, which plagued the area at the time and killed 10,000 Philadelphia people in the late 1700s.

Strawberry Mansion

East Fairmount Park
Philadelphia, PA 19131
(215) 228-8364

Strawberry Mansion is the largest mansion in Fairmount Park—although its original owner, Judge William Lewis, had actually planned it to be a simple country house. True, when it was built in the late 1700s, the home only consisted of the original middle section (a subsequent owner later added the two large Greek Revival wings on the ends). However, something tells me I could have done quite nicely with the original "simple country house." Originally called Summerville, the home became a popular restaurant in the nineteenth century. One of its specialty dishes was strawberries and cream, thus earning the home its nickname. The home is furnished with pieces from Federal, Regency and Empire styles that were popular at various periods throughout its ownership. The attic is filled with toys—but, to my kids' disappointment, they have antique toys that are to look and not touch.

Chapter Six

Woodford

33rd and Dauphin Streets
Philadelphia, PA 19132
(215) 229-6115

Woodford
Fee: $3
Hours: Tues-Sun 10 am-4 pm
Directions: Located next to Strawberry Mansion in Fairmount Park.

Built in 1756, Woodford is one of the oldest surviving examples of late Georgian architecture in the Philadelphia area. From the moment you step through the nine foot high entrance doors, you really get a feel for what it was like to be a member of the eighteenth century upper-class, as the home remains fully furnished with expensive pieces from that period. To me, the highlight of this building is the fireplace and mantle in the parlor—the intricate carvings obviously required a lot of time and patience.

Laurel Hill Mansion

East Fairmount Park
Philadelphia, PA 19106
(215) 627-1770

Laurel Hill Mansion
Hours: July-Dec, Wed-Sun 10 am-4 pm
Fee: $3
Directions: From Mt. Pleasant, turn left onto Randolph Drive.

Francis and Rebecca Rawle built this brick mansion among the laurel trees in the 1760s. Once perfect symmetrical, the house has undergone several additions (for example, after Francis died and Rebecca remarried, she added a kitchen wing). Only the mansion's main floor is open to the public. Keep an eye out for the great detail in the fireplace area, as well as the home's beautiful tile work.

Fun Facts

- Laurel Hill was confiscated by Pennsylvania authorities during the Revolution because of the Loyalist sympathies of Rebecca's second husband. She later bought the house back again.

- Dr. Philip Syng Physick (known as the father of American surgery) eventually acquired the house and left it to his daughter, Sally Randolph. The Randolph's sold it to the city for $68,000 in 1869.

To the West

Lemon Hill Mansion

Lemon Hill & Kelly Drives
Philadelphia, PA 19130
(215) 232-4337

Robert Morris, one of the signers of the Declaration of Independence and a good friend of George Washington, built a farm and greenhouses in 1770 on a 350-acre tract of land in the spot now known as Lemon Hill. Back then, it was known as "the Hills," but it soon earned its enduring nickname once residents observed the lemon trees thriving in the greenhouses. By 1798, Morris's finances had taken a nosedive and he was sentenced to debtors' prison. Henry Pratt bought the property and built the present Lemon Hills mansion, a perfect example of fine eighteenth century architecture. I loved the house before I even got through the door—the entrance features a pair of stairs that meet at the door, and a fanlight and sidelights surround the doorway. The home's interior features oval rooms, curved doors, several fireplaces and wonderful antique furnishings. My kids also love the entrance hall's "checkerboard floor" made of Valley Forge marble.

Lemon Hill Mansion
Fee: $3
Hours: Apr-Dec, Wed-Sun 10 am-4 pm
Directions: Follow Kelly Drive to the end of Boathouse Row. Make a right and go up the hill.

Horticulture Center

Horticultural Drive
Philadelphia, PA 19104
(215) 685-0096

The Horticulture Center includes twenty-two acres of beautiful greenery and plant life, as well as a greenhouse and butterfly garden. It also offers some great bird watching opportunities.

Horticulture Center
Hours: daily, 9 am-3 pm
Directions: Take Belmont Mansion Drive past Belmont Plateau and stay to the left.

Manayunk/Chestnut Hill

Located about six miles northwest of Center City, Chestnut Hill is like a laid-back suburb, and strives to be very kid-friendly. About a mile or so away, Manayunk is a former "mill town" which recently made a major effort to reinvent itself as a tourist hotspot. It has a "hip" vibe, with lots of funky clothing boutiques and bars that are hopping until the early morning hours. While the focus is more on young adults, there are some spots that would interest families.

> **Manayunk/Chestnut Hill**
>
> Directions to Chestnut Hill: Take I-676/Vine Street Expressway West to I-76West/ Schuylkill Expressway to Exit 340A (Lincoln Drive). Follow Lincoln Drive to dead-end at Allens Lane. Turn right onto Allens Lane and follow to dead-end at Germantown Ave. Turn left onto Germantown Avenue. Follow two lights into Chestnut Hill shopping district.

Edward Savaria Jr/Philadelphia Convention & Visitors Bureau

To the West

Woodmere Art Museum

9201 Germantown Avenue
Philadelphia, PA 19118
(215) 247-0476
www.woodmereartmuseum.org

This small art museum is housed in a renovated Victorian mansion in Chestnut Hill. Once the home of Charles Knox, the museum (which also includes a carriage house and six acres of grounds) provides lots of activities and programs for kids.

Woodmere Art Museum

Hours: Tues-Sat 10 am-5 pm;
Sun 1 pm-5 pm;
Closed Mondays

Ages: 6 and up

Cost: Adults $5;
Children (under 12) Free

Directions: Take I-676/Vine Street Expressway West to I-76West/ Schuylkill Expressway to Exit 340A (Lincoln Drive). Follow Lincoln Drive to dead-end at Allens Lane. Turn right onto Allens Lane and follow to dead-end at Germantown Ave.

For instance, the grounds have child-size colorful garden sculptures—the carriage house holds classrooms for children's art classes and there is even a dedicated Children's Gallery displaying art by and for children. The Children's Gallery features colorful paintings, small sculptures, and many prints—displayed at just the right height for little eyes.

Deshler-Morris House

5442 Germantown Avenue
Philadelphia, PA 19144
(215) 596-1748

This home was nicknamed the "Germantown White House" because George Washington lived

Deshler-Morris House

Hours: Apr-Dec, Tues-Sat from 1 pm-4 pm

Cost: $1.00 adults, .50 children

Directions: take Germantown Avenue north a few blocks from Grumblethorpe. The Deshler-Morris House is across from Market Square.

here from 1793 to 1794 to escape the yellow fever plaguing Philadelphia. (At that time, Philadelphia was the capital of the country.) The President's bedroom is on the second floor.

Chapter Six

Ebenezer Maxwell Mansion

200 West Tulpehocken Street
Philadelphia, PA 19144
(215) 438-1861

Guided tours exhibit the role of parents, children and servants in the mid-nineteenth century. Children may try out antique toys and household items.

Wyck

9201 Germantown Avenue
Philadelphia, PA 19144
(215) 848-1690

Wyck was built in 1689, and kids like to check out the toys and other belongings in the oldest family home in Germantown.

Ebenezer Maxwell Mansion

Hours: Apr-Dec, Sat-Sun from 1 pm-4 pm

Cost: $4.00 adults, $2.00 children, $3.00 senior citizens

Directions: Take Germantown Avenue to Tulpehocken Street and make a left.

Wyck

Hours: Apr-Dec, Tues, Thurs, and Sat 1 pm-4 pm, or by appointment

Cost: $3.00 adults, $1.50 children

Directions: Take Germantown Avenue to the intersection with Walnut Lane.

To the West

Other Places of Interest

Children's Park

Germantown Avenue
Philadelphia, PA 19118
(215) 248-6604

Kids love this large, colorful, climbing and playing paradise! A variety of wooded structures, complete with kid-friendly slides, tunnels, and swings keep children occupied for hours. I like the fact that wood-chips and rubber matting provide for a soft landing. While the kids have a ball, parents can take a much needed break on the benches.

Children's Park
Hours: Daily, dawn to dusk
Cost: Free

Morris Arboretum

100 Northwestern Avenue
Philadelphia, PA 19118
(215) 247-5777
www.upenn.edu/morris

This is a nice peaceful place to take a break from the city activity. Kids love the seasonal Garden Railway Display—model trains running through a village of miniature buildings, tunnels, and waterfalls. I like the Japanese Overlook, a tranquil Japanese rock garden. Swan pond is also a bit hit with the kids.

Morris Arboretum
Hours: Mon-Fri 10 am-4 pm; Sat-Sun 10 am-5 pm (Apr-Oct) Daily 10 am-4 pm (Nov-Mar)
Cost: Adults $6; Students $4; children under six are free
Directions: Located in the University of Pennsylvania campus.

Chapter Six

Schuylkill Center

8480 Hagy's Mill Road
Philadelphia, PA 19128
(215) 482-7300
www.schuylkillcenter.org

The Schuylkill Center offers a variety of outdoor and indoor natural history and environmental science programs for all ages, with family programs featured on weekends. The Center's 500 acres of land includes fields, forests, ponds and a wetlands area. There are six miles of hiking trails—most of which aren't too challenging for kids. Take Widener Trail (it's paved) to the Widener Bird Blind. Feeders are stocked all year—so you can be pretty sure of spotting at least a few birds whenever you visit.

> **Schuylkill Center**
>
> Hours: Mon-Sat 8:30 am-5 pm; Sundays 1 pm-5 pm
>
> Cost: Adults $3; Children $2
>
> Directions: Take the Schuylkill Expressway to Roxborough/Manayunk Exit (#338). Cross over Schuylkill River. Follow Green Lane to Ridge Ave. and turn left. Follow Ridge Ave. for 2 miles to Port Royal Ave. and turn left. Pass Pearlman playing fields and turn right on Hagy's Mill Rd. SCEE is about 1/2 mile down on left.

Smith Memorial Playgrounds and Playhouse

Reservoir Drive at 33rd Street
Philadelphia, PA 19103
(215) 765-4325

A great place to let kids have fun! One of my kids' favorite parts is the wide, wooden slide on which several kids can slide down side-by-side. The playground also includes a small pool, a carousel and swings. The playhouse offers all kinds of fun and activities for children twelve and under. Kids under five can visit the miniature city of "Smithville."

> **Smith Memorial Playgrounds and Playhouse**
>
> Hours: Playground Mon-Sat 9 am-4:45 pm (Closes 4pm Nov-Feb); Playhouse hours Mon-Sat 10 am-3:30 pm
>
> Ages: infant to 12
>
> Cost: Free
>
> Directions: Take 33rd Street north, then make a left on Oxford Ave.

To the West

Historic Bartram's Garden

54th St. and Lindbergh Blvd.
Philadelphia, PA 19143
(215) 729-5281
www.bartramsgarden.org

Bartram's is America's oldest botanical garden. This forty-five acre paradise features an old farmhouse, a river trail, water garden, large trees, and wetlands. A great place for a relaxing stroll, the park also offers a great view of the Schuylkill River, plenty of bird observation, a ball field, and playground. Take the house tour and see first-hand where the nine Bartram children lived. The water garden provides great goldfish watching. My kids always grab a copy of the kids' map to find hot spots of fun within the garden. We always look for the Franklinia tree (usually at full bloom in late summer), which the Bartram family personally saved from extinction.

Historic Bartram's Garden
Hours: Daily, 10 am-5 pm. Closed major city holidays
Cost: Free (House tour: adults, $5; kids, $3)
Directions: Take 23rd St. heading south to Gray's Ferry Ave. (crossing Market and South streets). Bear right onto Gray's Ferry Ave. and follow across Schuylkill River, taking first left onto Paschall Ave. Turn left at next light onto 49th Street and follow trolley tracks past sign for 54th Street. Make a sharp left turn into Bartram's Garden just beyond Amoco station, 54th St. sign, and railroad bridge (entrance is not visible until after bridge).

Chapter Six

Where to Eat

Bredenbeck's Ice Cream Parlor and Bakery

8126 Germantown Avenue
Philadelphia, PA 19118
(215) 247-7374
www.bredenbecks.com

Kids love this Victorian-style ice cream parlor and bakery, where they can enjoy sundaes, milk shakes and other cool treats. Don't forget to stop by the bakery and pick up some Philadelphia-style butter cookies.

> **Bredenbeck's Ice Cream Parlor and Bakery**
>
> Hours: Bakery: Mon-Sat 7 am-7 pm; Sun 8 am-5 pm Ice Cream Parlor, Daily 12 pm-9 pm
>
> Directions: Take I-76 Exit 32, Lincoln Drive. Follow Lincoln Drive to Allen's Lane. Turn right on to Allen's Lane Follow until you come to a T (Germantown Avenue). Turn left on to Germantown Avenue Bredenbeck's is located on the left, 1 block past the third light.

Where to Shop

Down 2 Earth

4371 Main Street
Philadelphia PA 19128
(215) 482-4199

All natural and recycled clothes, gifts and accessories.

> **Down 2 Earth**
>
> Directions: Take 76 to the Belmont Avenue/ Green Lane exit (Exit 31). Turn onto Green Lane, cross the bridge across the Schuykill Expressway, and turn right onto Main Street.

Restoration Hardware

4130 Main Street
Philadelphia, PA
(215) 930-0300

Specialty home furnishings store. A wide variety of home décor and accessories, as well as furniture, hardware, tools and gadgets.

> **Restoration Hardware**
>
> Directions: Take 76 to the Belmont Avenue/ Green Lane exit (Exit 31). Turn onto Green Lane, cross the bridge across the Schuykill Expressway, and turn right onto Main Street.

Chapter Seven

Outside the City

Edward Savaria Jr/Philadelphia Convention & Visitors Bureau

Heading West

Valley Forge National Historic Park

Valley Forge, PA 194841
(610) 783-1077

> **Valley Forge National Historic Park**
>
> Hours: Daily, dawn to dusk
> Visitor's Center—8:30 am-5 pm
> Closed Christmas Day
>
> Cost: Free, but some buildings
> have a small charge
>
> Directions: I-76 to exit 25.
> Follow N. Gulph Rd. for 2 1/2 miles to
> Visitor's Center on left

American Helicopter Museum

1220 American Blvd.
West Chester, PA 19380
(610) 436-9600
www.helicoptermuseum.org

> **American Helicopter Museum**
>
> Hours: Wed-Sat 10 am-5 pm;
> Sun 12 pm-5 pm
>
> Cost: Adults $6; Children $4

The Museum features nearly fifty helicopters and exhibits that span the history of rotary wing flight.

Kids love the helicopters they can actually climb into. Two 2-seaters have rotors that tilt, and the rescue copter has room enough for several copilots to "take flight" together.

Liberty Aviation Services, Inc., in cooperation with the Museum offers helicopter rides every Wednesday through Saturday from 1:00 p.m. to 3:00 p.m. in good weather. No appointment is necessary. Rides are on a first come, first served basis, and cost $30 per person. In addition, the museum offers half hour and hour-long sightseeing rides to Longwood Gardens, Valley Forge, and Philadelphia. Costs vary for these extended rides.

Outside the City

Pennsylvania Renaissance Faire

Mount Hope Estate and Winery
Cornwall, PA 17016
(717) 665-7021
www.parenaissancefaire.com

Medieval theme park complete with period costumes, jousting, juggling, storytelling, glassblowing, and more.

Strasburg Railroad

Route 741
P.O. Box 96
Ronks, PA 17572
(717) 687-7522
www.strasburgrailroad.com

A really relaxing and pretty ride—climb into an old converted train and take a forty-five minute tour through the Amish countryside.

Amish Village

Route 896
Strasburg, PA 17602
(717) 687-8511

You can see all the aspects of Amish life, from school to farming.

Pennsylvania Renaissance Faire

Hours: August to Labor Day—Sat-Mon 10 am-6:30 pm, Sept to first week in Oct-Sat and Sun, 10:30am-6:30 pm

Cost: Adults $21.95, child $7.95, age 5-11, under 5 free

Strasburg Railroad

Hours: Varies with season
Check website

Cost: Adults $9-$13; Children (3-11) $4.50-$9.50, (under 3) $1

Amish Village

Hours: Nov-May weekends, house only 10 am-4 pm, June-Oct daily 9 am-6 pm

Cost: $5.50 ages 13 and over, $1.50 children 6-12, under 6 free

Chapter Seven

Sturgis Pretzel House

219 East Main Street
Lititz, PA 17543
(717) 626-4354
www.sturgispretzel.com

Everything you ever wanted to know about pretzels and their history.

Sturgis Pretzel House

Hours: Mon-Sat,
9 am-5 pm
Last tour at 4:30 pm

Cost: $2.00 adults and children, under 2 free

Plantation Estates/Bed & Breakfast/Trail Riding

405 Throne Road
Fawn Grove, PA 17321
(866) 382-4171
www.padutch.com/z/plantationestates.htm

Bed & Breakfast that also provides guided horse trails.

Plantation Estates/Bed & Breakfast/Trail Riding

Cost: $40.00/person for 1 1/2 hour guided trail rides. Reservations required.

Toy Train Museum

300 Paradise Lane
Strasburg, PA 17579
(717) 687-8976
www.800padutch.com/z/toytrain.htm

A museum of toy tinplate trains—fun for kids of all ages!

Toy Train Museum

Hours: May-Dec,
Daily 10 am-5 pm;
weekends in Apr,
Nov and Dec

Cost: Adults $2.75, $1.50 children, under 5 free

Outside the City

Dutch Wonderland

Route 30 East
Lancaster, PA 17602
(717) 291-1888
www.dutchwonderland.com

A quaint amusement park geared toward younger children.

Sight & Sound Theatre

Route 896
Strasburg, PA 17579
(717) 687-7800
www.bibleonstage.com

Inspirational live stage productions of bible stories, complete with hundreds of performers and live animals—Noah's Ark, Daniel, and the Christmas Story.

Plain and Fancy Farm

3121 Old Philadelphia Pike
Bird-in-Hand, PA 17505
(717) 768-4400
www.padutch.com/z/plainandfancy.htm

A great place to take a break and eat while visiting Amish country.

Chapter Seven

Aaron & Jessica's Buggy Rides

3121 A Old Philadelphia Drive
Bird-in-Hand, PA 17505
(717) 768-8828
www.amishbuggyrides.com

Three mile buggy rides (sleighs available in winter).

Elmwood Park Zoo

1661 Harding Blvd.
Norristown, PA 19401
(610) 277-3825
www.elmwoodparkzoo.com

This zoo may be smaller than the big city varieties, but it's perfect for young kids. There are more than 150 wild animals, ranging from bobcats to prairie dogs.

Aaron & Jessica's Buggy Rides

Hours: From Mar-Nov, Mon-Sat, 9 am-dusk; Dec-Feb, 10 am-4:30 pm Closed Sundays

---

Elmwood Park Zoo

Hours: Daily, 10 am-5 pm

Ages: 2 and up

Cost: Adults $6.50; Children (2-12) $4.50

Outside the City

Going South

Brandywine River Museum

U.S. Route 1 & PA Route 100
Chadds Ford, PA 19317
(610) 388-2700
www.brandywinemuseum.org

This former grist mill now contains many of Andrew Wyeth's famous works, but the real attraction is the river nearby. There are also statues of animals, which of course kids love to climb on. There are also walking trails, a model train display, and a restaurant.

Brandywine River Museum
Hours: Daily, 10 am-4:30 pm
Ages: infant to 13
Cost: Adults, $5; Children (6-12) $2.50, (under six) free

Linvilla Orchards

137 W. Knowlton Road
Media, PA 19063
(610) 876-7116
www.linvilla.com

Linvilla Orchards
Hours: Daily, 9 am-6 pm
Cost: Free

There aren't too many working farms left in Delaware County, but this is a masterpiece, complete with apple orchards, petting zoo, and playground. The octagonal barn recently burned to the ground, so a barn-raising was held not long ago to replace the building.

Tyler Arboretum

515 Painter Road
Media, PA 19063
(610) 566-9134
www.tylerarboretum.org

One of the oldest and largest arboreta in the area, this property features 650 acres of trails, ponds, and streams. Kids love to run on (and roll down) the hills.

Tyler Arboretum
Hours: Daily, 8 am to dusk
Cost: Members free; adults $5; Youth (3-15) $3; children under 3 free

Chapter Seven

Longwood Gardens

Route 1
Kennett Square, PA 19348
(610) 388-1000
www.longwoodgardens.org

Longwood Gardens features 1,050 acres of gardens, woodlands, and meadows, twenty indoor gardens, thousands of different types of plants. Naturally, kids gravitate toward the Children's Garden, with its maze and mushroom-shaped fountains.

Longwood Gardens

Hours: Daily 9 am-5 pm; extended hours seasonal and during holidays

Cost: Adults $12; Youths (16-20) $6; Children (6-15) $2, (under 6) free

Directions: Take I-95 South to Route 322 West (Exit 3A) to Route 1 South.

Larry Albee/Longwood Gardens

Outside the City

Daniel Boone Homestead

400 Daniel Boone Road
Birdsboro, PA 19508
(610) 582-4900

Visit the place where Daniel Boone grew up (coonskin cap is optional).

Boomers

1056 Gap-Newport Pike
Avondale, PA 19311
(610) 268-5678
www.boomers4fun.com

This is a kid's paradise! No matter what your age, you'll feel like a kid again here. There's an indoor skate park, miniature golf, bumper boats, a driving range, virtual reality golf and more. Plus, pizza and ice cream!

Delaware Museum of Natural History

4840 Kennett Pike
Wilmington, DE 19803
(302) 658-9111
www.delmnh.org

An interactive museum packed with activities kids will love. There's a mini-theater, the Discovery Room featuring hands-on archeological activities and lots more.

Daniel Boone Homestead

Hours: Tues-Sat, 9 am-5 pm, Sun 12 am-5 pm Closed holidays

Cost: $4.00 adults, $2.00 children (6-17), under 6 free. Grounds free

Boomers

Hours: Sun-Thu 10 am-8 pm; Fri-Sat 10 am-9 pm Closed Mondays

Ages: 1 and up

Delaware Museum of Natural History

Hours: Mon-Sat 9:30 am-4:30 pm; Sun 12 pm-4:30 pm

Ages: 1 and up

Cost: Adults $5; Children (3-17) $3; Children (2 and under) Free

Chapter Seven

Up North

Herr's Snack Factory

Route 1 and 272
Nottingham, PA 19362
(800) 523-5030

This tour takes you through the complete process of making potato chips, pretzels, and other snacks, from raw materials to finished products. Free snack samples. Call ahead for reservations.

Crystal Cave

963 Crystal Cave Road
Kutztown, PA 19530
(610) 683-6765
www.crystalcavepa.com

Largest operating cave in Pennsylvania. Tour and see an interactive video. There is also a miniature golf area and gift shop.

Hershey

100 W. Hershey Drive
Hershey, PA 17033
(800) HERSHEY
www.Hersheypa.com

One of my kids' favorite places is the beautiful town of Hershey, where the light poles are shaped like chocolate kisses, and the entire town seems to smell like cocoa.

We always start our visit at Chocolate World, where you take a ride through the "Chocolate Factory" and learn all about the Hershey's company and how chocolate is made. The best part? You get a free mini chocolate bar after the ride!

Herr's Snack Factory

Hours: Mon-Thurs 9 am-2 pm, Fri 9 am-11 am

Cost: free

Directions: Take I-95 South to Route 322 West to Route 1 South. Exit Route 272 (Nottingham) and turn left. Travel for 50 yards, turn right onto Herr Drive and follow signs to the Herr's Visitor Center.

Crystal Cave

Hours: 9 am-5 pm daily, longer hours on some weekends

Cost: $8.50 adults, $5.00 children (4-11), under 4 free

Hershey

Directions: Right off I-81 (take the Hershey exit).

Outside the City

Hershey Park

100 Hershey Park Dr.
Hershey, PA 17033
(800) HERSHEY
www.Hersheypark.com

Hershey Park

Hours: May-Aug and Sept weekends 10 am daily, closing time varies between 6 am-11 pm

Cost: $24.95 age 19 or older, $15.95 3-18, ages 2 and under free. This price includes admission to Zoo America and to this amusement park.

Zoo America, North American Wildlife Park

Park Avenue
Hershey, PA 17033
(800) HERSHEY
www.zooamerica.com

Some examples of animals here are: alligators, black bears, elk, and bison. More than 200 animals in the eleven-acre park setting.

Zoo America, North American Wildlife Park

Hours: Daily 10 am, various closing times

Cost: included in admission to Hershey Park. Otherwise, $4.75 adults, $3.50 children 3-12, under 3 free. Animals and plants from five regions of North America.

Crayola Factory

30 Centre Square
Two Rivers Landing
Easton, PA 18042
(610) 515-8000
www.crayola.com/factory

Kids love the Crayola Factory. They can watch crayons and other art products being made; plus they can do a lot of fun projects and crafts.

Crayola Factory

Hours: Tues-Sat 9:30 am-5 pm; Sun 12 pm-5 pm Summer; Mon 9:30 am-5 pm

Cost: $8

Chapter Seven

Hawk Mountain Sanctuary

1700 Hawk Mountain Road
Kempton, PA 19529-9449
(610) 756-6000
(610) 756-6961
(610) 756-4468 fax
www.hawkmountrain.org

Spectacular trails for bird watching, particularly during hawk migration in the fall.

Hawk Mountain Sanctuary

Hours:Trails open dawn to dusk. Visitor's Center 9 am-5 pm daily Closed Thanksgiving, Christmas and New Year's Day

Cost: Visitor Center is free; hiking trails $4.00 adults, $2.00 children 6-12, under 6 are free

Bushkill Falls

Bushkill Falls Road
Bushkill, PA 18324
(717) 588-6682
www.bushkillfalls.com

Bushkill Falls

Hours: Apr-Nov, 9 am to dusk

Cost: free

There are many scenic trails surrounded by gorgeous scenery and numerous waterfalls. On display are exhibits of American Indian artifacts as well as animals native to North America and Pennsylvania.

Outside the City

Knoebel's Amusement Park

Route 487
Bysburg, PA 17824
(800) ITS4FUN
www.knoebels.com

Knoebel's Amusement Park

Hours: Varies with season, weekday/end—check website or call

Cost: varies according to time of day

This is one of my favorite family attractions. For one thing, there is no admission charge. You buy ride tickets and pay as you go, or pay a flat fee to get a "hand stamp" valid for the whole day. One of the things I hate most about amusement parks is that Jack and I usually have to pay full-price, even though we spend most of our time waving to our kids as they zoom past on the rides. At Knoebel's, we don't pay a dime for ourselves—well, except for the seventy cents in ride tickets to ride the Pioneer Train, which we do as a group every time we go.

Here's the other thing I love about this place—family bathrooms! Meaning, you can have a private bathroom all to yourself and your young kids. As the mom of three boys, I never quite knew what to do when my boys were younger and had to go to the bathroom. I didn't feel right about letting them go to the men's room alone, yet I hesitated to take them into the ladies' room with me, lest I make them (or the other women) uncomfortable. Of course, they're old enough to use the men's room solo now, but the family bathrooms are still useful; when I have young nephews or other kids with me.

Chapter Seven

Fonthill Museum

East Court Street & Route 313
Doylestown, PA 18901
(215) 348-9461
www.fonthillmuseum.org

Betcha didn't know there was a real castle in Pennsylvania, did you? Well, there is—and it has forty-four rooms, eighteen fireplaces, and more than two hundred windows!

> **Fonthill Museum**
>
> Hours: Mon-Sat 10 am-5 pm;
> Sun 12 pm-5 pm
>
> Cost: Adults $7;
> Children (6-17) $2.50

Sesame Place

Oxford Valley Road
Langhorne, PA 19407
(215) 757-1100
www.sesameplace.com

Your preschoolers and young kids will be in heaven at this amusement theme park with Sesame Street characters. There's no bigger thrill for a toddler than running into Bert and Ernie!

> **Sesame Place**
>
> Hours vary by season—
> call for hours,
> generally 9 am-5 pm
>
> Cost: $21.95 per person
> includes all rides and shows;
> under 2 free. $4.00 parking

East to NJ

You can actually walk over the Ben Franklin Bridge to get to New Jersey. It's a nice walk, with great views, but may be too long for younger kids.

Note
Camden, N.J. has some rough neighborhoods, so it's best to stick to the main streets and not venture far from the tourist spots.

Outside the City

New Jersey State Aquarium

1 Riverside Drive
Camden, NJ 08103
(856) 365-3300
www.njaquarium.org

Brandon's favorite animal is the penguin, so he loved watching them waddle around here. My kids also like the shark tank.

New Jersey State Aquarium

Hours: Winter hours
Mon-Fri 9:30 am-4:30 pm;
Sat-Sun 10 am-5 pm. Summer,
daily 9:30am-5:30 pm Closed
Thanksgiving, Christmas Day,
and New Year's Day

Cost: Adults $12.95;
Children (3-11) $9.95,
(under 3) free

Kelly Mooney/ NJ State Aquarium

Storybook Land

Black Horse Pike
Cardiff, NJ 08232
(609) 641-7847

The park has rides for younger children, animals to feed, and many shade trees for hot summer days.

Storybook Land

Hours: Summer,
daily 10 am-5:30 pm
Call for hours in
late spring and Oct-Dec

Cost: $9.50 per person,
under 1 free

Chapter Seven

Wheaton Village

1501 Glasstown Road
Millville, NJ 08332
(800) 998-4552
www.wheatonvillage.org

Watch glassblowers at work, visit the Glass Museum, or just buy some treats at the penny candy general store.

Wheaton Village
Cost: $8.00 adults, $5.00-$7.00 students/seniors, under 6 free
Hours: 10 am-5 pm, varies by season, Apr-Dec-daily, Jan-Feb; Fri-Sun, and Mar; Wed-Sun

Canoeing/Tubing/Rafting/Camping in the N.J. Pine Barrens

Camping and canoeing in the Pine Barrens varies in cost—free if you have your own canoe and tent! The cheapest way to go is to shop around at the local rental shops. Many rental companies will meet you at the end of your destination and drive you back to your starting point. Here are some rental companies:

- **Pine Barrens Canoe Rental**, Chatsworth—(609) 726-1515
- **Wading Pines Campground**, Chatsworth—(609) 726-1313
- **Paradise Lakes Campground**, Hammonton—(609) 561-7095
- **Mick's Canoe Rental**, Chatsworth—(609) 726-1380

Barnegat Lighthouse State Park

P.O. Box 167
Barnegat Light, NJ 08006
(609) 494-2016

The Barnegat Lighthouse State Park is located at the northern most tip of Long Beach Island, New Jersey. The thirty-two acre park is home to the Barnegat Lighthouse as well as a variety of shore and migratory birds. The park is open all year and there is no cost for parking or entering the park.

USS New Jersey

62 Battleship Place
Camden, NJ 08103
(866) 877-6262
www.ussnewjersey.com

The Battleship New Jersey is on the Delaware River in Camden, N.J., directly across from Penn's Landing. You can take the River Ferry to get to the battleship.

USS New Jersey
Hours: Seven days/week, Oct-Mar; 9 am-3 pm, Apr-Sept; 9 am-5 pm
Cost: $10 adults, $7.00 children under 12

Chapter Eight

Calendar

January

Mummer's Parade

Starting 8:00 a.m. on New Year's Day and lasting several hours, this parade features thousands of marchers adorned in elaborate costumes while festive music blares in the background. Parade starts at 5th and Market and proceeds around City Hall.

February

Black History Month

Many special films and exhibits are presented at the African American Museum on Arch Street. Call (215) 574-0380 for details.

Chinese New Year

Watch for the celebrations, including huge banquets, to start in late February. Contact the Chinese Cultural Center at (215) 923-6767 for more details.

March

Philadelphia Flower Show

You definitely don't need a green thumb to appreciate the beautiful displays, colorful floral creations and basically anything flower-related you can possibly imagine that will be on display. This is the nation's largest flower show, featuring acres of exhibits. Held at the Pennsylvania Convention Center at 12th and Arch Streets. Call (215) 988-8800 for more information.

Rob Ikeler/Pennsylvania Horticultural Society

Calendar

St. Patrick's Day Parade

Parade begins at noon at 20th and the Parkway on the Sunday closest to St. Patrick's Day. Needless to say, Irish pubs in the area are packed during and after the parade.

The Book and Cook

Sponsored by the Food Network, this event pairs food critics, cookbook authors, and other culinary "experts" with prominent local chefs—to see what tasty delights their collective imaginations can dream up. Usually held toward the end of the month, this event features wine tasting and food samples galore. Call (215) 965-7676 for more information.

April

Philadelphia Antiques Show

For more than four decades, this annual event (held the first weekend of the month at the 103rd Engineers Armory at 33rd and Market) has drawn antique lovers from across the country. Call (215) 387-3500 for more information.

Easter Sunday

Enjoy fashion shows and other celebrations (featuring an appearance by a certain long-eared bunny) in Rittenhouse Square on Easter Sunday.

Fairmount Park Spring Tour

Usually held the last Sunday of the month, this event features special trolley tours of the park's wooded areas, with most of the trees in full bloom. Call (215) 636-1666 for more information.

Chapter Eight

Philadelphia Open House

Beginning in late April and continuing until mid-May, this is your opportunity to get a rare glimpse inside some of the area's beautiful private homes, gardens, and historic buildings, which are usually not open to the public. Call (215) 928-1188 for details.

May

Dad Vail Regatta

On Mother's Day weekend, the largest collegiate rowing event in the country is held here. Enjoy some family time in Fairmount Park, where you'll have a great vantage point to watch up to 500 shells from more than 100 colleges race up the Schuylkill River.

Jim McWilliams/Philadelphia Convention & Visitors Bureau

Calendar

International Theater Festival for Children

Held the last weekend of the month on the University of Pennsylvania's Walnut Street campus. Call (215) 898-6791 for information.

Jam on the River

This festival (held on Memorial Day weekend) has a New Orleans attitude and a focus on families having fun. Held at Penn's Landing, the event features jazz and blues music as well as great food.

Devon Horse Show

If your kids are animal lovers like mine, they'll love this event (held at the end of the month on Rt. 30 in Devon, outside Philly) featuring horse races, jumping competitions, and other horse-related activities. Call (610) 964-0550 for details.

June

Head House Square Crafts Fair

Held on weekends throughout the summer, the craft fair allows local artists, craftsman, and other vendors to show off and sell their creations. Located in the area of Second and Pine Streets. Call (215) 790-0782 for more information.

Elfreth's Alley Days

During the first weekend in June some residents of Elfreth's Alley graciously open up their homes for public viewing. Check out the re-enactments of colonial crafts and activities, and admire the residents' colonial costumes. For more information, call (215) 574-0560.

Chapter Eight

Rittenhouse Square Fine Arts Festival

The festival runs for the first two weeks in June, and features hundreds of works of art created by local professional and student artists. Call (215) 634-5060 for information.

Pro Cycling Championships

This competition, held the first weekend in June, includes a 156-mile course that starts at the Parkway and the forces competitors to bike the grueling hills of Manayunk.

July

Sunoco Welcome America Festival

Needless to say, Philadelphia—especially Old City—really comes to life in early July. If you can bear the heavy crowds, it's a great time to visit. The Sunoco Welcome America Festival is a weeklong event, celebrating America's birthday with lots of free entertainment (including several big concerts), a reading of the Declaration of Independence, lots of official ceremonies and a lighted boat parade. Festivities occur at various spots throughout the city, including Independence Hall, Penn's Landing, and the Philadelphia Museum of Art. Don't miss the fireworks extravaganza on the Delaware River on July 3rd. For more information, call (215) 636-1666 or visit www.americasbirthday.com.

Calendar

August

Pennsylvania Dutch Festival

During the first week of August, visit the Reading Terminal Market and enjoy the crafts, food, music, and other offerings of the Pennsylvania Dutch.

September

Philadelphia Distance Run

Usually held the third Sunday of the month, this half-marathon features thousands of runners and a thirteen-mile course across the city. If your kids are the athletic type, let them see how they fare in the children's run.

October

Columbus Day Parade

The parade on South Broad Street is held on the second Monday of the month.

Super Sunday

On the third Sunday of October, a huge celebration takes place on the Benjamin Franklin Parkway. Look for clowns, mimes, jugglers, rides and more. Call (215) 665-1050 for details.

Chapter Eight

Terror Behind the Walls

For the last two weeks in October, the Eastern State Penitentiary holds this Halloween-themed event, featuring a spooky tour complete with actors in scary costumes. Call (215) 236-3300 for more information.

November

Philadelphia Museum of Art Craft Show

Usually held the second weekend of the month, the craft show features exhibits by more than 100 of the top crafters from across the country. Call (215) 763-8100 for information.

Thanksgiving Day Parade

The parade on Benjamin Franklin Parkway features lots of incredible floats, as well as thousands of marchers.

December

Various Holiday Happenings

Lots of special holiday events take place this season throughout Philadelphia. Society Hill and Germantown host Christmas walking tours, the Pennsylvania Ballet performs "The Nutcracker" at the Academy of Music, the awesome "Private Lights" event is held on South Colorado Street, and a Swedish pageant called Lucia Fest is held in South Philadelphia.

New Year's Eve Fireworks

Held at the Great Plaza in Penn's Landing.

Edward Savaria Jr/Philadelphia Convention & Visitors Bureau

Chapter Nine

Index

A

B

C

Index

Index

Index

M

N

Index

S

Index

If you enjoyed the
CITY OF BROTHERLY LOVE,
you'll love THE BIG APPLE!
Did you know that Manhattan is less than four hours from downtown Philly? Check out these sample pages from *A Parent's Guide to New York City*.

The Bronx

Manhattan

Queens

Brooklyn

Staten Island

New York City

Chapter Two

What To Do
with Children In New York

Bettman/Courtesy Empire State Building

From as far as New Jersey across the Hudson and Queens across the East River, the Empire State Building dominates the New York skyline.

Landmarks

Landmarks come in many shapes and sizes, and the nature of their appeal ranges as widely. Some are so visibly or palpably cool—or so very famous—that any child old enough to talk will be thrilled by them. Others require more sophistication to be fully appreciated. This section lists New York's best-known and most significant sights, with a special emphasis on what's likely to appeal to the younger members of your party, starting with the five most famous.

The Big Five: New York's Signature Sights

The Empire State Building

350 Fifth Ave. at 34th St.
New York, NY 10118
212/736-3100
www.esbnyc.com

B, D, F, N, Q, R trains
to 34th St. and Sixth Ave.;
#1, 2, 3, 9 trains to 34th St.-Penn. Station;
#6 to 33rd St. and Lexington Ave.

Observatory open 9:30 a.m.-
12 midnight daily.
Observatory admission: $7 adults, $4
seniors and children 5-12, free for
children under 5. Snack bar at 86th fl.
observatory. Wheelchair accessible.

"New York Skyride," 2nd level,
212/279-9777; open 10 a.m.-10 p.m.
daily, separate admission: $11.50
adults, $8.50 children 4-12.

The world's tallest building—wow!
That's what my five-year-old
thought as he craned his neck out
the bathroom window of our
Greenwich Village apartment to
catch a glimpse of the 102-story,
1,224-foot Empire State Building.
Seeing it from our apartment was an
everyday satisfaction, as opposed to
the thrill of taking the long elevator
ride up to the 102nd-floor observatory and seeing four states! Eighty
miles in every direction!

Edwin Steussy

It's not the world's tallest anymore, and as of this writing, the observatory on the 102nd floor is closed. But the view from the one on the 86th floor is nothing to sneeze at—forty miles in every direction on a clear day—and the Empire State Building is still a required stop for every family that visits New York. During the forty-plus years it held its title, it came to symbolize both the city and 20th-century progress, a meaning it still carries.

When the building opened on May 1, 1931, it was remarkable for more than its height. The nation was mired in the Great Depression, and the building's great expense was a gesture of optimism made visible in its bold, modern Art Deco lines. Nothing topped it until 1972, when the World Trade Center opened its 1,350-foot-tall twin towers at the southern end of Manhattan. The World Trade Center held the title for a scant two years, losing it in 1974 to Chicago's Sears Tower.

Today the Empire State Building is (only) the world's seventh tallest (the tallest, at 1,483 feet, is the Petronas Tower in Kuala Lumpur, Malaysia), but it remains emblematic of New York City, as the Eiffel Tower is of Paris—the sight you can see from practically anywhere in New York. Try to time your visit for a sunny day or clear evening to get the best of the view.

The New York Skyride, a separate attraction on the building's second level, offers a gimmicky 20-minute interactive "simulated space-ship ride" over and under the city, but at a rather hefty price—$11.50 for adults, $8.50 for kids. You might be better off passing up the virtual tour for more of the real.

Every night, all year round, the top of the building is bathed in colored spot-lights, the colors changing week by week in observance of various events on the city's calendar. Red and green at Christmas time; red, white and blue on July Fourth; the colors of the city's athletic teams when any team is in the running for a championship. As mentioned above, the building is visible from much of Manhattan, and the lights are actually easier to see at some distance away.

The Statue of Liberty and Liberty Park

Liberty Island (in New York Harbor, south of Manhattan)
New York, NY 10004
212/363-3200
www.nps.gov/stli

N, R, #1, 9 trains to South Ferry; #4, 5 trains to Bowling Green.

Open 9:00 a.m.-5:15 p.m. (later in summer).

Admission free; ferry ticket $7 adults, $6 seniors, $3 children 16 and under (a.m. ferry departures frequent, later departures up to every half-hour or 45 min.). Elevator to top of pedestal only; inside of statue not wheelchair accessible.

Joseph Pobereskin/Courtesy NYC & Co.

The Statue of Liberty was a nation's welcome sign when poet Emma Lazarus wrote, in "The New Colossus," "Give me your tired, your poor, your huddled masses yearning to breathe free..."

There isn't a child in the country—for that matter, in the world—who doesn't recognize the image of the green colossus in New York Harbor. For more than a hundred years, it's been a symbol of the United States. That's why it's both a National Monument and a World Heritage Site.

Popularly known as "Lady Liberty" and "the Lady with a Lamp," the statue—perhaps the most famous one on Earth—is officially named "Liberty Enlightening the World." When poet Emma Lazarus called it "the new Colossus" in her famous poem of the same name—the one that ends, "I lift my lamp beside the Golden Door"—she was referring both to its moral stature and its actual size: 152 feet on an 89-foot pedestal. It was sculpted by Frederic-Auguste Bartholdi on a frame designed by Alexandre Gustave Eiffel (yes, the man who designed the Eiffel Tower) and presented to the United States by France in 1886.

You can take a ferry there and climb to the famous torch—or you can just admire it from a distance from the southern tip of Manhattan. If you do go there, Liberty Park, which surrounds the statue, provides an oasis of quiet from the sometimes too-intense city. In the summer, you might want to relax in the park before climbing the 354 steps to the top (there is no elevator)—until your fellow boat passengers descend, reducing the body heat inside. You don't have to go back on the next boat out.

Times Square

42nd-44th Sts.
(between Broadway and Seventh Avenue)
New York, NY 10018

1, 2, 3, 9, R, N, and S trains
to 42nd St.-Times Sq.;
B, D, F, Q, trains to 42nd St. and Sixth Ave.;
A, C, E trains to 42nd St. and Eighth Ave.

Open 24 hours. Free admission.

Brian Pasternak

Disney's *Beauty and the Beast* is typical of the entertainment available in the new, reformed Times Square.

A giant straw pops in and out of a giant Coke bottle, a giant cup of coffee steams real steam, a giant TV screen shows the news while two giant "zippers" run the headlines, and a giant map displays the time in cities around the world. The signs that made Times Square famous still dazzle, the first time and every time. Times Square isn't a square; it's two triangles formed by the intersection of Broadway and Seventh Avenue.

Times Square was named the Crossroads of the World for the intersection. Broadway was named the Great White Way when the night-banishing neon signs (now mostly replaced by even shinier digitized screens) that surrounded the "square" were unique.

At mid-century the area began to decline, and by the 1980s it was filled with triple-X movie theaters and sex shops, although Broadway theater continued to flourish to the east and west of the "square." Then New York City and the Disney Company entered into a partnership to rehabilitate Times Square, a process now largely completed. A few porn theaters and stores still linger along Eighth Avenue a long block away from Times Square, but the Square itself is squeaky clean. Many of the old movie houses have been refurbished and are now presenting live musicals like Disney's The Lion King. Some New Yorkers liked it better the old way, but there's no doubt it's more family-friendly now.

Staten Island Ferry

South Ferry
New York, NY 10004, and St. George
Staten Island, NY 10314
718/815-BOAT
www.SI-web.com/transportation/dot

Runs 24 hours, seven days, every 15 min.
rush hours, less frequently other times.

Free. Wheelchair accessible.

Hear the cry of the gulls and the ferry's foghorn blare, smell the salt tang of the sea, watch the great ships and garbage scows ply the water—you're about to take New York's own magical mystery tour, the ride across New York Harbor on the Staten Island Ferry. Ahead rise the green hills of the quiet Staten Island community of St. George, and out of the water to your right rises the great green Statue of Liberty. Magic indeed—and free, as magic should be.

"We were very young, we were very merry/We went back and forth all night on the ferry," wrote the young Greenwich Village poet Edna St. Vincent Millay in the 1920s. It was a simpler era, and the nation's youth, even in sophisticated Greenwich Village, sought simpler— or at least less technologically advanced—pleasures. The twenty-minute ride (each way) on the ferry recaptures that simplicity for the whole family.

There's been a ferry between Staten Island and the southern tip of Manhattan since 1817, when railroad magnate Cornelius "Commodore" Vanderbilt branched out by running a ship called *The Nautilus* across the harbor. (At the time, of course, it was the only way to go—no bridge had tamed the harbor yet, nor would one for nearly 70 years.) New York City took over operation of the ferry in 1890. By that time, there was a bridge across the East River, but not yet one going to Staten Island. The ferry is still the only direct route between Manhattan and Staten Island, but you now see no fewer than four bridges in the course of the round trip: on the southbound ride, the immense Verrazano Narrow Bridge between Brooklyn and Staten Island and, in the distance, the Goethals Bridge connecting Staten Island and New Jersey; heading back, the Brooklyn and Manhattan Bridges over the East River.

It's that ride back that gets everyone. In the words of the anonymous writer in what may be the best New York City guide ever written, *The WPA Guide to New York City*, "Manhattan's slender shafts seem to rise out of the water in one solid pyramiding mass. When night conceals the shoreline, the illuminated towers seem suspended in the dark."

From the sublime to the pedestrian: The ferry is the only Metropolitan Transit Authority-operated facility that has rest rooms and a snack bar that sells the ubiquitous New York hot dog, required eating on the ferry ride for all but vegetarian passengers. (There are also rest-rooms in the terminals at both ends of the ride, if you can't bear to miss a minute of the view.)

Brooklyn Bridge

**City Hall Park in Manhattan
to Cadman Plaza, Brooklyn**
www.endex.com/gf/buildings/bbridge/bbridgelinks

#4, 5, 6 trains to
Brooklyn Bridge-City Hall
in Manhattan; A, C trains to High St.-
Brooklyn Bridge in Brooklyn.

Walkway is open at all times.
Wheelchair accessible.

Of all New York's signature sights, the Brooklyn Bridge may be the least immediately impressive to a child's eye; many will have seen larger and more dramatic bridges. If you want them to enjoy it, you may have to explain that when it opened in 1883, it was one of the wonders of the world.

It was not only the first bridge to cross the East River and the first suspension bridge to use steel cables; at 6,016 feet, it was then (and remained for the rest of the century) the longest suspension bridge anywhere. Long eclipsed as an engineering feat, it remains beloved today for its beauty and for the spectacular views from its pedestrian walkway.

Its history is equally powerful. It took thirteen years for German-born engineer John O. Roebling to persuade the two cities (Brooklyn and New York) to attempt to build a bridge; it took another thirteen years to build it. But Roebling never saw its spires rise from the water. Shortly after work commenced in 1870, an accident on another construction site crushed his foot, and he died of tetanus. His son, Washington Roebling, took over the helm of the project, but was himself disabled by an accident only two years into the bridge's construction, in 1872. He continued to oversee the project from his Brooklyn Heights townhouse.

In 1983, New York put on one of its most lavish public celebrations ever for the Bridge's centennial. Today, energetic Brooklynites commute over it on foot and bicycle; for a different perspective on the city you're visiting, you might want to join them.

Living History

Apollo Theater

253 W. 125th St.
(between Adam Clayton Powell and Frederick Douglass Blvds.)
New York, NY 10027
212/749-5838

Victor Erdosh

The Apollo!

#2, 3, A, B, C, D trains to 125th St.

Tours $8.

The endless list of legendary African-Americans who have appeared on the Apollo's fabled stage since 1934 includes everyone from Duke Elllington and Billie Holiday to James Brown, B.B. King, and Wynton Marsalis, to Lauryn Hill. (1934 was when the Apollo reopened as a vaudeville house—it was originally built for burlesque in 1913.) Its luster dimmed in the 1970s, but was renovated in 1986 and still hosts its famous Wednesday evening Amateur Nights, Wynton Marsalis' Jazz for Young People series, and more.

Bowne House

37-01 Bowne St.
Flushing (Queens), NY 11354
718/359-0528

#7 train to Main St.

Undergoing restoration; visits by appointment only. Wheelchair accessible.

When the Dutch still ruled New York, an English Quaker family named Bowne settled in what is now Flushing. They had left England for Holland and then America seeking religious freedom, only to be persecuted here by intolerant adherents of the Dutch Reformed Church. Eventually they won their struggle, and the Dutch agreed to permit Quaker worship. John Bowne built this farmhouse in 1661; Society of Friends founder George Fox preached across the street in 1672; William Penn slept here in 1700.

A Parent's Guide to
School Projects

ISBN: 1-931199-08-6

Price: US$17.95 (CAN$26.95)

• **Children in today's public and private schools face far different requirements than their parents faced just a generation ago.** Today's classrooms require more homework (at an earlier age), a more highly developed sense of design and creativity, and more commitment of time and effort from students and parents. Nothing reflects this change more than the growing reliance on project-oriented teaching.

• **A Parent's Guide to School Projects introduces parents to this new educational world.** Beginning in Kindergarten, students are required to put together a variety of projects, from the familiar Science Project to interesting alternatives to the book report. Author Kathie Weir shares insights gained from her experience coaching her own children through scores of projects. Her experience as an educator allows her to offer perspective from the other side.

• **The book features examples of successful projects in several subjects** including Science, History, English and Geography. Kathie also offers tips and general guidelines on writing research papers and putting together effective student presentations.

• **The new emphasis on projects is not limited to those designed for individual students.** Group Projects are increasingly popular with teachers as a way to introduce students to group dynamics. A Parent's Guide to School Projects offers advice on how to avoid the most common pitfalls. Among these are lack of coordination among participants and the unfortunate occasions when a minority of the membership ends up doing the majority of the work.

• **Classroom projects tell only half the story.** Just as teachers seek ways to enhance and enliven classroom activities, teachers and administrators try to encourage closer parent involvement beyond helping their children with their homework. From field trip chaperone to Parent Teacher Association President to sponsoring after-school activities, parents are offered plenty of opportunities to help in both public and private schools.

• **As Public Schools strain to meet increasing demands on limited resources, they've come to rely upon a variety of fundraisers to help defray their costs.** Kathie's been involved in dozens of these fundraisers, and she offers advice and guidance for every level of participation — parents helping their children sell 'School Spirit knick-knacks' and those proposing and coordinating entire fundraisers will benefit.

• **Sometimes fundraising is not enough** — public schools appreciate contributions of expertise and experience from everybody in the community as a way to enrich learning. A Parent's Guide to School Projects explores these possibilities for greater involvement, from giving a talk on 'Career Day' to organizing a three-day 'Harvest Festival' to teach city children about farm life.

• **An appendix collects sample project assignments** — contributed by elementary and middle school teachers.

• **Indexed for easy reference**. Includes a glossary.

About the Author: Kathie Weir, mother of a 12-year-old and 14-year-old, has spent the last nine years coaching her children through increasingly complex school projects, papers, and presentations. She has served as a PTO board member, helped out in the classroom, and coordinated scores of fundraisers and extra-curricular activities. Her experience as an active volunteer parent and substitute teacher has brought her into contact with dozens of dedicated public school teachers, many of whom contributed project assignments as well as their insight. Kathie is also the author of **A Parent's Guide to Los Angeles** and has published numerous articles and essays about children and child rearing.

parent's guide press

PO Box 461730
Los Angeles CA 90046
phone: 800-549-6646
fax: 323-782-1775

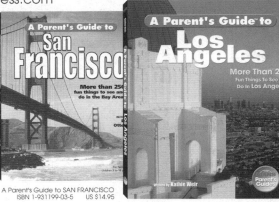

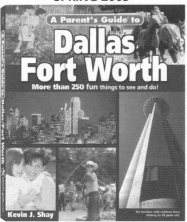

A Parent's Guide to
Money

ISBN: 1-931199-19-1

Price: US$19.95 (CAN$29.95)

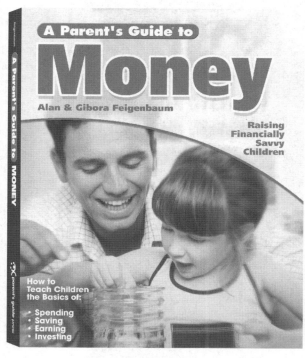

• **The collegiate class just entering the job market** carries the highest level of student and credit-card debt ever, even considering inflation. These recent graduates will have to learn for themselves how to responsibly manage money, but there's plenty of time to ensure that kids growing up today can enter adulthood better prepared than their older siblings were.

• **Financial writer Alan Feigenbaum,** with the help of daughter Gibora, shows how to view children's financial development the same way a parent might view their growth stages – the financial equivalents of crawling, standing, then walking. Picture-book to checkbook, car seat buying to buying that first car, *A Parent's Guide to Money* leads parents through the necessary baby steps on the road to family financial success.

• **How parents can prepare their personal finances** when they're expecting. Starting with difficult questions about false, 'pre-conceived,' assumptions about managing money, and where those may have been learned, Alan helps parents get their pre-child finances under control in preparation for keeping the same control after baby has arrived.

• **When to introduce children to financial concepts** – from the first piggy bank through investing in mutual funds. Once infants understand that money is more than something to put in their mouths, it's time to start teaching them what money is, what it's for, and how to control it (rather than it controlling them later).

• **Tips and strategies** to teach children what they need to know about the four basics: Spending, Earning, Saving, and Investing. The thorough discussions of these four topics make clear many financial concepts many parents may themselves be confused about. The authors then provide scores of intriguing suggestions about how and when to teach the same concepts to children.

• **A thorough Resource Appendix** leads readers to scores of online resources – games, calculators, and in depth information – all reviewed by the authors for accuracy and relevance.

• **Indexed**.

parent's guide press

PO Box 461730
Los Angeles CA 90046
phone: 800-549-6646
fax: 323-782-1775

A Parent's Guide to
First Aid

ISBN: 1-931199-20-5

Price: US$17.95 (CAN$26.95)

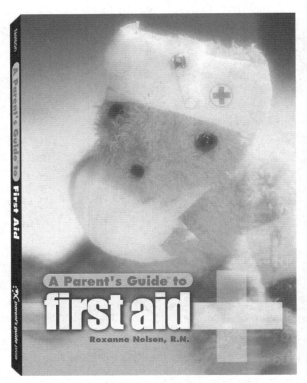

- **When something goes wrong**, Parents and Caregivers are often the first ones on the scene. Knowledge of fundamental First Aid principles can be vital for the health of children. While nothing can replace qualified First Aid training, this book can provide an essential reference in time of need.

- **Common childhood mishaps** are listed in alphabetical order – from Allergic Reactions to Vomiting – for quick reference. Symptoms and causes are clearly explained by former pediatric and newborn intensive care nurse Roxanne Nelson to help caregivers understand the situation.

- **Step by step instructions** help caregivers determine the appropriate level of care and when to seek it – from a call to 911 in the direst circumstances or giving First Aid that can be undertaken at home.

- **Accident prevention** is the best First Aid one can give. The book includes common sense prevention tips for each situation, as well as general safety precautions parents can take around the home.

- **Chapters devoted to CPR/Rescue Breathing**, the Heimlich maneuver, and the emergency medical system each help parents and caregivers learn the basics before a crisis arises – helping them stay calm and in control of the situation.

- **What to stock in an effective home First Aid Kit**, where to keep it, and how to keep it up-to-date.

- **Indexed**.

 **parent's guide** press

PO Box 461730
Los Angeles CA 90046
phone: 800-549-6646
fax: 323-782-1775